s 7/89

3

$3

AFRICAN BACKGROUND

THE TRADITIONAL CULTURE OF THE SHONA-SPEAKING PEOPLE

by

MICHAEL GELFAND

WITH A CHAPTER BY
THE REV. FATHER M. HANNAN, S.J.

JUTA & COMPANY, LIMITED

CAPE TOWN   WYNBERG   JOHANNESBURG

1965

First Published . . . . December, 1965

℗ PRINTED IN SOUTH AFRICA BY THE RUSTICA PRESS, PTY., LTD., WYNBERG, CAPE.

FOREWORD

by WALTER ADAMS, C.M.G., O.B.E., B.A. (Lond.), Hon. LL.D. (Malta and Melbourne). Principal, University College of Rhodesia and Nyasaland

Professor Michael Gelfand has already won for himself an international reputation in several fields by his contributions to clinical medicine, to the history of medicine and to medical sociology. In this present book, he carries further his studies of the Shona peoples to whose service so much of his career has been devoted.

It is written with the sympathy and insight that characterize all his work and provides a picture of the traditional Shona family and village before the changes caused by Western influences. The traditions, beliefs and behaviour which he describes persist not only in the changing rural, but also in the urban situations in which the 'Africans' find themselves today. Knowledge and understanding of these factors are essential to any analysis or interpretation of the contemporary scene in Rhodesia, and to the shaping of personal relationships in political, economic or social life.

Whatever else Professor Gelfand has done in this study— and he does much more—he shows how irrelevant it would be to interpret Shona society and behaviour by the assumptions of individualism implicit in Western thought and attitudes. In his conception of property and personal riches, the Shona traditionally is not the economic man of an acquisitive society. Politically the Shona man or woman cannot be abstracted from the social context which is a part of his or her being. Edmund Burke described the State as 'a partnership not only between those who are living, but between those who are dead and those who are to be born'. In Shona society, as Professor Gelfand describes it, this interdependence of the generations is a fact of daily experience.

The intensity of the loyalties, obligations and fears within the Shona family or village units produced a cohesion which opposed the individualist, the eccentric and the abnormal. In this sense, its demanding conservatism and conformism made the African, in Professor Gelfand's words, the most 'normal' of men.

The atomization of Shona societies is now destroying the traditional norms. The migration of men in the working period of their lives to the mines, industries, towns and farms; the changes of attitudes resulting from mission and other Western education; the penetration of the rural areas by urban influences and by the creation of new economic 'needs' and practices—these, and many other factors, are transforming the social structures, the beliefs and the behaviour patterns which Professor Gelfand describes. The traditional world, however, endures both in social practice, and, still more, in the minds of men and women. It is the great merit of this study that Professor Gelfand describes with sympathetic understanding the Shona society which is part of living history, knowledge of which is essential to all of us who are concerned with contemporary Africa.

I know that it will be the reward that he most wants for his patient labours in producing this book that we who read it should share the affection and understanding which inspire this vivid portrait.

PREFACE

This study deals principally with the behaviour of the Shona. In it I have tried to depict his character and personality, for knowledge of his joys and sorrows must go a long way towards understanding his philosophy of life. How often have we heard the comment, 'If only I knew what the African thinks!' and this book is an attempt to answer this problem in as an objective a manner as possible.

Valuable research on African custom and thought has been done by social anthropologists, missionaries and others and now this knowledge is beginning to take shape and become much clearer in our minds. Perhaps the line I am following may be a useful one for others to try. This is not necessarily a subject to be explored only by the white man. The African himself must realize that there is much in his culture which is sound and beautiful and which can be an example to Western peoples if only they know about it. In this age of materialism an attempt to follow some of the ideals of the African would be of great benefit to other nations.

This subject should be closely studied by members of my own profession because successful practice depends on a good understanding of our patients. With this object in mind we have instituted a course of lectures, which we have called 'medical anthropology' for the first year medical students at the University College of Rhodesia and Nyasaland.

I could not have written this book without the help of the Rev. Father Hannan S.J. who patiently corrected my text at all its stages and was also kind enough to contribute a chapter of his own. Dr. B. Granger, Mr. Charles Noon, Mrs. G. V. N. Barlow, M.B.E., Dr. V. N. Barlow and my wife were very helpful with their criticisms and useful suggestions.

University College of Rhodesia
and Nyasaland   MICHAEL GELFAND
Salisbury

CONTENTS

Chapter   *Page*

1 Introduction 1

2 The Shona People 5

3 The Family 9

4 Defined Duties in the Family 21

5 Friendship in Shona Society 46

6 Manners 60

7 Procedure 72

8 The Fear of Witchcraft 94

9 Language and Culture
  by the Rev. Father M. Hannan, S.J. . . . 102

10 The Spiritual Concept 107

11 Normal Behaviour and Attributes . . . 119

12 Concluding Thoughts 124

THE AUTHOR ACKNOWLEDGES THE ASSISTANCE GIVEN BY
THE RHODESIA STATE LOTTERY TRUSTEES

Introduction

Many people speak enthusiastically about Africa as a
great continent. Some are attracted by its gold, copper or
diamonds, others by its raw materials. Many more are
interested in its vast open spaces peopled by tribes some
'traditional' others emergent. Many are excited at the
prospect of a tour or a flying visit to catch a glimpse of the
Victoria Falls, the Kruger National Park or one of the game
reserves of Kenya or the Congo.

More prefer to come as visitors than as settlers. Some look
at the continent with political eyes, trying to devise means of
keeping the masses under the influence of the Western
world or conversely deciding how to link them with Russia
and her satellites. Doctors who come to Africa are greatly
impressed with the vast amount of clinical material so
easily accessible. They have but to lay a hand on a sick
African and a new observation can be made. The industrialist
or business man sees good prospects and even riches ahead.
He finds immense possibilities in this sphere. He can put
up factories to be run with relatively cheap labour and thus
with the promise of a good return.

There is also a fair sprinkling of Europeans who come to
this continent such as the great missionaries of the past
—David Livingstone, James Stewart, Robert Moffat, Robert
Laws, Father Daignault and many others—to bring a new
way of life, a new religion, a new way of behaviour to its
peoples. Many with the same missionary zeal and spirit of
sacrifice still exist today. What better example can I give than
that of Albert Schweitzer? These men and women exemplify,
too, the virtues of goodness, charity and sacrifice, seeking no
reward save bringing Christianity and all it embraces to the

African. We cannot travel anywhere in any part of Africa without stumbling across a mission station.

Many love Africa for its warmth and its sunshine—even in wintry weather. Others cannot forget the smell of the first rains, bringing with them a sense of rejuvenation. After the great heat and dryness, day after day, when we are driven almost to despair, the dark clouds gather and the heavens open, bringing a new feeling of freshness and a promise of survival to the land and all on it.

Africa is full of attractions. Its sun and brightness cannot be equalled. Life is rough for many, especially those living far from the towns. Yet modern facilities are available even to them.

Life is still exciting in Africa, but perhaps the most stimulating part of all is the European saying, 'What does the African think about?' or 'Once we know what is in the African's mind we shall know what to do'. Others again are confident that they truly understand the African. After spending years among them they are ready to tell any visitor about Africa and its people and pose as authorities on its future. They can sometimes speak a sort of dialect or a few words of 'pidgin Bantu' and have wielded a certain amount of authority over their African staff. But in reality they are not experts on Africa. They may be fond of the African and get on well with him—but they are the bosses. Although they are careful not to interfere with the life of the African in his village or his sleeping quarters, when something goes wrong with their lands, businesses or homes they suddenly flare up and hot words fly. After a little while, perhaps within a few minutes, tempers subside and hurts are forgotten. Master and servant seem to forget the upset and, as if nothing had happened, each returns to his routine until the next storm. We are often amazed at the calm maintained by the African during such outbursts and the fact that he seems to bear so little grudge. He takes the admonition well in a dignified manner without signs of emotion, almost as if there was nothing personal in the whole affair.

Most men who can claim they know something of Africa admit, on closer questioning, that the African's mind is a mystery to them. Many Europeans, even if they do not say so openly, wonder whether the African is a normal human being; if he has the same drive. I have often heard it said: 'Why was it that when we came here they had no wheel, no chair, no reservoir?' An American professor of pathology with a good reputation, highly respected in medical circles, recently stated that the American Negro is not equal to the white man in brain capacity. I am certain many people attribute this to lack of opportunity, but there are quite a number who maintain that, all things being equal, the African is inferior and we cannot expect great things from him. This does not mean that these critics do not like the African. It is possible to be superior to another person and yet be fond of him, willing to stand by and protect him and to offer him material assistance and kind advice. Others admire the African, believing that he is exceptionally capable provided he is given the opportunity.

To most Europeans the African remains an unknown quantity. There is hardly a white man who does not inwardly believe that the African knows secrets about life and death. Almost every week I am told of wonderful cures wrought by witchdoctors, who will not let a white person into these closely guarded secrets. They say they have certain cures for madness, fits, rheumatism, growths and snake-bite —all conditions that baffle the medical profession. We observe the wonderful sense of rhythm of the African who lets himself go in traditional society in a way no white man can emulate. Many Europeans are impressed by the apparent brilliance or outstanding ability of a particular African, born and brought up in a hut, who later passes difficult examinations in English and finds his way to a university where he graduates in law, arts or medicine. This shows that rich latent talent lies hidden and is released under certain circumstances. All these observations go towards making the African a subject of amazement and bewilderment to us.

In this study I shall endeavour to describe some aspects of

the behaviour of the African in the traditional environment of his village and discuss the forces that dominate his life and outlook. An understanding of Shona background helps to an understanding of the individual. If I can do this creditably, I believe I shall have justified the many days spent with the Shona and also pay tribute to a people unsurpassed in many of the virtues prized so highly by European society and who have the further advantage over some of the other African tribes of having lived and occupied Rhodesia for at least 1,000 years continuously.

It would be true to say that the person who is rich, who has many material advantages over others will tend to place himself in a superior position or attitude to the one whom he regards as less fortunate. Thus the great diversity between the average European and average African in material resources is so striking that many a European is made to feel superior whereas the African, aware of his material contrast, may consider himself less fortunate and, therefore, inferior. Yet such a difference is only a measure of wealth or of resources. It is not a measure of the character, emotional stability or state of contentment of the individual. It is certainly no yardstick with which to judge ability, trustworthiness, kindness and other qualities. The European is, perhaps, apt to assume that, because of the much greater material benefits he enjoys, he is superior in all other respects to the African. He therefore concludes that he is mentally superior—a deduction which lacks proof and smacks rather of the application of the principle of symbolism.

2   *The Shona People*

This study is concerned with the traditional African, or should I say the Shona who have only had very slight contact with European culture. They continue to cling strongly to their own religious practices and for the most part are quite unacquainted or uninterested in Christianity. They all turn to the *nganga* when ill, although it does not follow that they oppose the help of a European doctor if it is close at hand. All of them believe strongly in their religious faith. They rest on the prescribed day of rest when no one is permitted to work in the fields. This day of *Chisi*, as it is known, corresponds to the Sabbath. When confronted with a serious problem, or when a death occurs, they are more than likely to turn to one of their ancestral spirits or to believe that the illness or death can be blamed on a witch. In a matter of tribal concern such as a lack of rain, they turn to their tribal spirits *(mhondoro)*. Each clan has its own *mhondoro* which comes through its human host or medium *(svikiro)* and speaks to the tribesmen seated around him. They listen carefully to the man so possessed, revealing the causes of the drought, or who should be the next chief and so on.

The Shona nation, about 3½ million strong, occupy the greater part of Rhodesia (except the south-western portion around Bulawayo where the much smaller Matabele nation lives). The Shona consist of four large segments or sections: the central Mazezuru living around Salisbury for a radius of 80 miles; the Makorekore, who are centred around Mt. Darwin to the north-eastern corner of the colony; the Manyika, who are concentrated around Umtali in the eastern districts and the largest section, known as the Vakaranga, who radiate from Fort Victoria. They are all Shona-speaking, and all are patrilineal, and for practical purposes favour the same interests and follow the same political structure. Essentially, the whole Shona tribe is divided into numerous clans, each clan bearing its own distinguishing totem, and they are all exogamous. It would be true to say that practically no marriages take place in which the man has the same totem and sub-totem as the woman. I regard this as a further sign of how closely the Shona are still wedded to their ritual beliefs. Marriage is a rather complicated affair in which the family of the suitor has to make certain payments to the family of the chosen girl. She then belongs to his family and will have a village to settle in—the village of her husband. The bridewealth does not belong to the girl's father but rather to the cognates, and when his son marries, it will be used to procure a wife for him.

Each clan is ruled by an hereditary chief or sub-chief, depending on the size of the clan or sub-clan. The chief's judicial powers have been considerably reduced since the European administration, but today he deals with minor cases, all concerned with native custom and practice. No cases of a criminal nature are judged by the chief. In this task the chief is helped by a simple court of four to six trusted men whom he appoints as his advisers. These men may or may not be his relatives, but they are wise men who can be relied on to express an able opinion on African customs, law and practice, and on land in the African trust lands (reserves). An application by a man to settle in the district falls within the chief's powers, but nowadays this is largely dealt with by the Administrator in consultation with his chief. An important duty of the chief, formerly, was to settle accusations of witchcraft, and even today it is correct to inform the chief that a charge of imputing witchcraft has been made by the complainant before the police of the district are notified.

What is so basic to an understanding of the Shona is the family structure of each village. The majority of the inhabitants of each village are related—a closely knit kinship group, headed by the father or grandfather, with his wife, sons, daughters and their families. Thus the size of the village varies enormously from a bare dozen people to as many as 100 or 200 relatives. Most of the larger villages will have one or perhaps more strangers—(*vatorwa*)—men outside the clan who have come to the village and asked for permission to live in their midst.

The husband and wife live in the main hut or *imba*. Here she cooks the food over the central fireplace. Here she keeps her cooking and eating utensils, and stores her clay pots on the potshelf. Here will be kept a large clay pot where the family can find drinking-water. At night the couple sleep, with their children up to the age of about 8 years, on reed mats on the floor. For older children each sex is given a hut to sleep in. An important structure within a few yards of the main hut is the granary where the grain is stored. Lying close to the wall of the *imba* will generally be found a grinding stone on which the mother, or her daughter, grinds the grain to flour. Larger grain such as maize she stamps to a smaller size first with a mortar and pestle. Also close to the hut and generally just on the periphery of the yard of the village is the *dare*, which simply consists of a few stones on which the men sit, talk and where, too, they are given their food by the women. Outside this yard, within 20 or 30 yards, one comes across the simple circular enclosure called the *danga* (cattle-pen) in which the cattle are kept at night.

Cattle are slaughtered for eating, but only rarely, and then for special reasons. Closely bound up with the Shona faith is the principle of sacrifice. Every family should, on one or more occasions, dedicate a bull to the memory of the spirit of the grandfather and the time generally comes when the spirit calls for the beast to be sacrificed in his honour. It is difficult to assess the number of cattle owned by the family units, but it may be said to be about five or six.

Essential to each *musha*, too, are the gardens, each about 2 to 4 acres in size, and here the husband and wife will plant the crops. Typically it is by hoe culture, but nowadays more and more use is made of the plough.

The main cereal crop is maize, but other popular ones are finger millet (popular for preparing beer), bulrush millet (*mhunga*) and rice; and monkey-nuts are grown throughout the territory. The main vegetables are pumpkin—especially the leaves—*bovora*, and sweet potatoes. In a typical Shona garden one finds more than one crop is planted, such as maize, *mhunga* and pumpkins. As a rule the seed is simply scattered.

A large village or, more usually, a varying number of related smaller villages are linked together under a headman (*sabuku*), who is the link between the villages and the chief. He, too, has certain duties such as the settling of any minor civil matters, but anything more important must be referred to the chief. The *sabuku*, who is appointed by the chief, collects the taxes from the villagers.

A typical show village in southern Mashonaland. People are gathered around the main hut (*imba*). Photograph taken in 1963. (see page 6.)

A family using the hoe (*badza*) in the traditional way. (Chikwaka reserve.) (see page 22.)

About to stamp the maize in a *duri*. (see page 33.)

Where the fowls are kept. (Kandeya reserve, northern Mashonaland.) (see page 7.)

3   *The Family*

One of the outstanding features of Shona life, which also determines to a great extent the behaviour of the individual, is the emphasis placed on the family unit. In European society we have lost the fixed mode of behaviour and as a result the family units are breaking up. The African family links are much stronger than in the European family, and the behaviour of each individual in his relationship to the rest of the unit is governed by most elaborate rules. We soon realize that the Shona family is a strong, closely knit unit with a powerful magnetic pull, drawing each one into its bonds. Each relationship is part of a complicated system. This family unit reminds me of a small fortress designed to protect and aid each person inside it, who also contributes towards the maintenance and sustenance of the rest. Each member of the African family has his own well-defined duties. He knows what he has to do, where and when it must be done, what not to do and—most important of all—never to offend the other members. The duties are laid down by a deeply ingrained tradition and are virtually impossible to change so long as the African lives in this atmosphere. They are followed as strictly as any religious ritual. Anthropologists remark on the strong ties of the family group. It does not follow, however, that everyone therein is blissfully happy, tensions and quarrels arise as in any society.

On analysis of the family structure we notice the different status accorded to each person. For instance that of the grandmother is different from that of the father or the grandfather. I am not wrong in saying that the grandfather *(sekuru)*—father of the husband—has the most honoured position in the family in the patrilineal society unless he is too old and feeble, when his eldest son assumes the position of dignity in the family. This does not mean that the rest of the family, especially the women, are not respected or given due consideration. The grandmother (mother of the husband) and the sisters of the husband each have their place and their rights and duties. Although a woman falls on her knees when handing her husband his plate of food, this is not a sign of serfdom, as the mother of the family has a very vital and real place in society. When her daughter marries she is recognized by the payment to her of a cow for the spirit of her mother (*mombe youmai*). This is entirely her property, and even today, when many customs are being discontinued, this payment is still made.

The strength of the family is fortified by the intimate bonds existing between the living and the spirits of their immediate departed relatives to whom they look for protection, support and guidance. Even in the spiritual world we notice the seniority and importance attached first to the departed grandfather (*sekuru*), then to his wife, next, to that of the father and, finally, to that of the mother. In other words in the eyes of the Shona, the family bonds are not broken by death, but the family has its spirit elders in the spiritual world. The older a person becomes, as his span of life draws to an end, the greater the respect and consideration he receives. The effect of this outlook has a special bearing on social relationships, for, instead of feeling a burden upon the younger members of the family, as each man or woman grows older, he (or she) feels secure in the knowledge that he is respected and revered by the young. How very different from European society, and even from the African society today in which traditional influences are disappearing.

As already mentioned the man is master of his wife and children, who acknowledge this. By paying bridewealth his family has acquired and owns her, yet, because she is his wife and mother of his children, she has a high and respected status. She is a partner in the family unit and, although her status is junior to her husband's, her share in the unit is vital for its happy and continued existence. She cannot be easily displaced and has to be considered. Her husband cannot interfere with the preparation of food. She has an interest in looking after the lands in the same way as he has. She is assigned her own plot on which to grow food and, although its produce is eaten by the whole family, her husband cannot sell any of it without her agreement. The question of ownership of property is complicated. The wife cannot be overruled by her husband's demands when the matter concerns her own granary. She can purchase cattle with her grain, although it is more correct, and certainly wiser, if she consults him first. He would buy the beast for her. If he refuses to agree she cannot proceed further, but he is more likely to accede as she is giving away her own grain in exchange for the animal. If the husband wants to purchase cattle, he is also expected to discuss the matter with his wife, although he can overrule her. Whenever the wife or children need clothing the husband takes grain from his own granary to purchase it. Her grain is used for food for the family unit and preparing beer but not for purchasing clothes. The wife also has certain rights over cattle she has earned from herding at her parents' village when she was a girl. These and their offspring belong to her and she can leave them to her children. Her husband cannot demand them for fear of annoying her family spirits and thus bringing illness upon his own children.

As she acknowledges her husband's superiority a mother is careful to teach her children to respect their father and listen to him in all matters. They dare not argue with him. No child is ever permitted to be rude to his father or mother, even though she assumes a lesser state of dignity than her husband. There is no doubt that this lesson is learnt early in the life of every Shona child, who is strictly disciplined and severely punished by his mother or father if he shows any lack of consideration to his parents or fails to carry out their instructions. Certainly by the time he is 7 or 8 years old he knows that certain members of the family have a special place in it and they must be accorded the respect due to them.

I have already mentioned the increased status an African acquires as he grows older until he reaches the stage of being a grandfather whose seniority is highest both in this and the next world. The most junior member of society is of course the grandchild, then the son or daughter, rising in importance to father, his father and finally his grandfather.

Father Hannan (personal communication) draws attention to those five social strata in ascending order of status from grandson to grandfather; but within the same stratum age and sex confer on an individual increased status or respect. He expresses this important principle as follows: 'Within each stratum the accident of priority of birth gives to boy or girl, to man or woman, the status of older brother or older sister (there is no word in the language for plain, unqualified brother, or sister). It is within the microhierarchy of brothers and sisters where the lesson is early learnt that membership in the family involves duties and rights. The younger must obey the older; the older has a right to the obedience of the younger. The older has a duty to protect the younger; the younger has a right to the help of the older.

'Again I would not suggest that anyone ever consciously thought this out, or even consciously accepted the principles, but, in fact, this interdependence, this surrender of independence, is the guarantee that the inadequate individual will not be overcome by the hostile elements of his or her environment.'

The effects on each stratified social group may be to restrict expression, for this system tends to perpetuate tradition with each of the strata subordinated to the one above it. Thus the junior strata must obey the senior ones. Perhaps this is another reason for the little change that has taken place in this society for centuries. Father Hannan believes that this system explains why we still witness today rituals recorded by the Portuguese in the sixteenth and seventeenth centuries.

But we must not forget that these strata of social groups

apply to the same family unit. Between families, not of the same blood, this seniority or increased social status is not necessarily accorded to age. For instance, a good example is the respect displayed by a son-in-law (*mukuwasha*) towards his father-in-law (*tezvara*), for, if his father-in-law were to die, he would still take a place subordinate to the latter's successor as head of the family no matter what his age. The eldest son of the father-in-law might be but a child yet the son-in-law must show his respect to him. Father Hannan only partially agrees that the great desire of the traditional Shona is to ensure equality as he has observed that no two individuals in the kinship grouping are equal socially or treated in exactly the same way. He refers to the particular kinship structure in these words: 'A person is either my relative or a non-relative; if he is a non-relative he is inferior to me (he may be richer or cleverer, but socially he is inferior). If he is a relative he is either superior to me or inferior; he may belong to the highest rank of my social world—males to whom I give the name of *vasekuru* and towards whom I adopt the behaviour pattern proper for me towards them, or females to whom I give the names *ambuya* (grandmother) or *vambuya* (mother-in-law).

'The person may belong to the social rank immediately above mine—that of males to whom I give the name *baba* and towards whom I adopt the behaviour pattern of *mwana* or that of females to whom I give the name *amai* and towards whom I adopt the appropriate behaviour patterns.

'The person may belong to the same social stratum as myself; if he is a male and was born before I was, he is superior to me. If he was born after I was he is inferior to me— the former I call *mukoma* and adopt the behaviour pattern of *mununguna* towards him. If he is younger I call him *mununguna* and adopt the behaviour pattern of *mukoma*. If the person is female, she is inferior. I call her *hanzvadzi* and adopt the behaviour pattern of *hanzvadzikomana* towards her.

'There are two social ranks inferior to me, those of *mwana* and of *muzukuru*. From this it is clear that, apart from twins whose order of emergence into the world is not known, there are no two people who are equal in Shona society.'

I agree that this form of inequality is found in the family relationships, but this is seen, although to a lesser degree, in European society where the eldest son regards himself as superior to his younger brothers. It is more a matter of seniority than of inequality. Outside the family circle, however, the same or equal status of 'citizenship' is enjoyed by all men in the clan bearing the same totem; quite different to the social or even monetary distinctions found in European society.

THE SUPREMACY OF THE MALE

Shona society is predominantly patrilineal and therefore the male is the accepted head of a family and his eldest son succeeds him[1]. His word is final in most matters and his decisions hold, as his wife and those dependent on him are bound to accede to his wishes. Of course he accepts the fact that his wife and other womenfolk have certain defined tasks, and whether or not he regards these as inferior to his own is immaterial. He does not interfere in the carrying out of these duties provided they are performed satisfactorily and leaves his wife to make her own decisions in these matters. But in certain others she must obey. For instance it is the man's right to have his sexual wants satisfied and the woman dare not argue with him on this score. It is not considered good for a man to lose his temper, but if he does and thrashes his wife, even if he is in the wrong this is his privilege.

The fact that a man, or rather his family, has paid for his wife, bestows on him the right to regard her and her children as his property and she knows this. In the event of a quarrel, or if she has not fulfilled her duty as a wife, or has committed adultery or some other disgraceful act, he can send her back to her father and expect him to return the bridewealth. When the girl's parents hand her over to her husband it is a *sine qua non* that she is a virgin and in all respects a good,

[1] The status of *vambuya* (mother-in-law) is evidence of matrilineal influence.

well-behaved and respectable woman. Yet on the other hand she can expect her husband to care for her and help her when it is his duty and if he is cruel, lazy or neglectful of his family responsibilities she is able to seek the protection of her father in which event he forfeits the return of any bridewealth. Although his sexual demands must be fulfilled he is not entitled to commit adultery and if he is unfaithful to his wife she may leave him and, although he is the master he has no right to ill-treat his wife or children. Whenever his wife is seriously ill the husband must inform her relations to avoid any possibility of being accused of causing her death by malnutrition or other neglect as he is responsible to her clan for her well-being. This is also the case among the Akan, Twi-speaking tribes of the Ashanti and Ghana although the clan is matrilineal.[2]

The father of a family unit is its first consideration. For example, his fields must be tended first, and although he helps in his wife's afterwards, he is not obliged to do so. No woman is accorded the privilege of sitting at the *dare* to eat or discuss matters, but if the husband wishes he may have his food in the hut, although he sits separately from the womenfolk.

Beattie (1958), describing the marriage and affinity of the Nyoro, mentions that the man is always of a higher status than the woman, who must always obey her husband. When they walk together she must follow a few paces behind. If she offends him, he is at liberty to beat her, but she still has her rights and in any serious disagreement the matter can be taken to her father. The wife must always be provided with a house, clothes and a hoe with which to dig and her husband must not fail in his duty towards her.[3]

It is only fair to the male to point out at this juncture that many male privileges are based not on his superiority but on his greater strength. For instance, men milk the cows because they are stronger and a certain amount of danger is associated with the handling of animals. Hunting and fishing

[2] Amoo, J. W. A. *Africa* (1946), *16*, 228.
[3] Gelfand, M. *Shona Religion* (1962), 131. Juta & Co., Cape Town.

are also considered dangerous occupations. Although the male is the ruler of the family and his position is undisputed, the wife has an acknowledged and responsible position. The crops she grows belong to her and her husband cannot sell any of her grain without her permission. No husband or son should purchase an animal, or any property, without first consulting his wife or mother. If she were opposed to this he could still overrule her, but the matter must at least be debated first.

The superiority of the male in Shona society extends to the spiritual world as well; the spirit of the grandfather takes first place and that of the grandmother comes next. Some say the father is more important, but this has not been my experience. A bull is dedicated only to the grandfather's spirit to which it may be sacrificed afterwards. This male spirit cares for the whole family group, which turns to it in times of emergency.

We notice this conception of male superiority in many of the rites carried out by the Shona. For instance when a widow accepts one of her husband's brothers at a ceremony called *nhaka*, she crawls towards him on her hands and knees with a calabash of beer. She tastes it and then hands it to him saying, 'You are my husband. I do not want to be beaten or have any nonsense from you.' Her acknowledge-ment of his authority to beat her implies that the man is the undisputed master of the family unit.

LOVE THY PARENTS

Almost every Shona reveres his parents. Not only does the child love them but he looks up to them and accords them proper respect. He listens to them, seldom argues with them and tries to avoid causing them pain. *Honour thy father and thy mother* is far stronger in Shona society than among Europeans. This is due to the belief that the parental in-fluence is close at hand even after death. The spirits of the dead parents and grandparents protect the living family. Thus any unkindness shown to a parent during his lifetime may mean the risk of punishment by his spirit, perhaps years after his death. Disrespect or disobedience towards them may thus recoil upon the person concerned, or on another member of the family.

An angered or aggrieved spirit that returns to punish the guilty person or his children is referred to as an *ngozi*, and every Shona child is taught that disobedience and disrespect to his parents may result in a visitation from such a spirit. There is a special ritual known as *kutiza botso* which is used to placate it. Let us imagine that a mother is grieved because one of her sons has beaten her, and this remains on his conscience. Years later, after her death, when he has married and begotten children of his own, one of them becomes ill and fails to respond to treatment. The family consult many diviners until one of them eventually brings to light the fact that the father actually hit his own mother when she was alive, and so establishes the diagnosis that the illness was caused by the paternal grandmother, whose spirit complains of this disgraceful act. Therefore amends must be made to the spirit so the child will recover. As the first part of the reparation the man must give an ox to his mother's spirit. Then he must take off his clothes and dress in old rags with pieces of blanket round his waist. In one hand he holds a small piece of calabash and in the other a larger portion. He then speaks to his mother's spirit saying, 'This is the ox I am giving' and leaves his village and visits all the neighbouring villages in turn begging for grain. At each place he publicly picks up a little sand in the small piece of calabash and blows it away saying, 'Grandmother, you left your snuff-box', thus admitting that he wronged his mother when she was alive. Everyone in the village makes fun of him and then gives him a little millet to put in the big piece of calabash. He journeys through many villages in this way, until he has collected about three bushels of grain, when he returns to his own home and brews beer from the grain he has brought back. A ceremony is held and he offers the beer and the ox to the aggrieved spirit to whom he thus makes reparation for his offence.

One of the surest ways of hurting a Shona is to swear at him by using disrespectful language about his mother. For instance, to say 'Your mother's vagina' immediately brings forth a violent emotional reaction resulting in rage and violence, as the most dear person in the world has been insulted. A parent is his very being—one who has lived for him, fed him and taught him—one to whom he is ever grateful.

As the parents become old their children's respect for them grows, because they will soon be in the next world where they exert considerable power over their offspring. Therefore no Shona is likely to show any unkindness to an elderly relative who is close to his end. Indeed Father Hannan (personal communication) considers it possible that, in the eyes of the Shona, the elderly are already living in the next world—spirits on earth. As a result the Shona tends to care for the elderly and ensures that they have means of sustenance, a hut to live in and a grandchild to help fetch and carry. The traditional Shona shows more concern for his elderly relatives than does the modern European family, who so often, for various reasons, send them to old peoples' homes or other institutions to avoid having to care for them. This could never happen in traditional Shona society.

Loving his parents involves more than a natural affection for them; it also includes a fear of their power in the hereafter. But, even in this conception, love is the predominant factor, as it is believed that the parents' love continues after death and protects the living from harm even though the protective spirits consider it necessary to mete out punishment for previous misdemeanours. Some Shona feel that the Christian religion is lacking in this respect as they think that Christians may only remember their dead in their prayers, but do not pray to them, and thus they do not gain the comfort that an African does, with the knowledge that the spirits of his dearly loved parents and grandparents—his only true friends—are hovering about his hut, his fireplace, his fields and cattle-pen.

THE DESIRE FOR CHILDREN

The Shona people, like many other African societies, display an intense desire to have children, and if a woman does not fall pregnant or give birth to a living child, her family goes to any lengths to find a remedy. To say whether this urge in the African is greater than in the European is difficult, as, in my experience, Europeans also are most concerned that their marriages should be fruitful. It is true that the European family tends to be much smaller than the African one, but this does not mean that the partners in a European marriage are not keen to have children. The two societies are different in their economic and social background, which accounts for the difference in the size of the families, but, at the same time, the European is often extremely upset if his marriage is childless or if only one infant is produced. If an African family is small this may be due to the high infant mortality. Indeed the death rate is so extraordinarily high that this great urge for many children may be the desire to compensate for coming losses. There is a good chance of losing an only child and a family with only two or three children may easily be severely reduced in strength under present conditions.

A probable powerful reason for the African's desire for dependants is that unless there are offspring a dead man's or woman's spirit will have no one to honour it. It is said that the spirit of an unmarried person is unimportant, and only when a person marries can his spirit in the hereafter hope to receive the respect due to an ancestral spirit (mudzimu). Unless there are children left behind, the spirits of the parents will have no one to offer them beer when they want it, and those of the father and grandparents will not be able to have a bull named after them nor have one sacrificed in their honour. The Makorekore seem to go even further in this respect as they pray only to the spirits of the grandparents. So for an individual to have full acceptance in the family and to ensure a happy hereafter, he should have grandchildren. It is said that the spirit can 'look down' from the spiritual world, join in the pleasures of the family left behind and derive much satisfaction when their children pray to them.

A person does not really feel he has proper status in society until he has grandchildren, for only then is he certain that he will not be neglected or forgotten in his old age and that when he is dead he will be remembered by the living.

Thus we can see the African living his life on this earth as an integral and inseparable part of his family circle, and passing into the next world as a spirit in close contact with his kin still alive. In contrast to this the European tends in his life to ensure where possible an individualistic approach, free from any close ties except with the closest members of his family. The African, too, maintains a closer ritual link with members of his clan than does the European who, while he might acknowledge and even be proud of his nationality, strives to maintain and preserve his personal independence and individualism.

4   *Defined Duties in the Family*

The Shona likes to know exactly where he stands in his family and community and what is expected of him. He does not like uncertainty nor does he seek a higher status than he is entitled to, or try to gain an unfair advantage over his fellow men. But he realizes that unless each man in the village knows precisely where his duties lie, trouble will ensue sooner or later and so he is much happier when he knows his and his neighbour's precise functions in the kinship group. This has all been worked out so that each person is taught his duties and knows his own status. The male has different duties from the female; the stranger (*mutorwa*) in a village, who does not belong to the kinship group, has specific duties of his own, so has the young married woman who has come to live in her husband's village with his family. All this has an effect on the behaviour of the group.

DIVISION OF DUTIES

Most typical of Shona life is the strict separation of the two sexes in their daily routine. The visitor is immediately struck by the well-defined duties of each sex, although some are shared by both and others are performed by one group, whereas we should expect them to belong to the other. For instance the floor of the hut is always smeared with dung by the women, yet when it is first constructed its walls can be smeared by either sex, but is mostly done by men. The reason for the distinction between these two duties is difficult to follow.

Broadly speaking there is a clear division of tasks between the male and female. Some are performed by men and others by women and this helps to keep the peace. No man cooks and no woman hunts, but some duties involve both sexes. For instance, work in the gardens is shared by them both, although the husband's garden is the primary concern and is the first to be tilled. When there is more than one wife all must help in the husband's field (*zunde*).

With the cattle, on the other hand, there is no overlap— this is the male's prerogative. He tends to do everything required for the upkeep of the cattle-pen and is solely responsible for the welfare of the animals. He milks, and the boys herd the cattle, although in families with no sons, or none available, the daughters may have to watch the cattle. While the men are responsible for the cattle the husband does not own them all, for his wife may have her own and the daughters, too, may have inherited some or, occasionally, have earned them as payment for herding. The mother is given a cow by each son-in-law when he marries a daughter; this beast and its offspring belong to her and she can kill it or sacrifice it to her spirit elders whenever she thinks proper.

This division of duties is inculcated into the children from very early years and even young boys and girls readily fall into line with the others. We notice that the women and girls gather firewood for the main hut but not for the *dare* where the men congregate as this is strictly a male affair. If we inquire a little more closely into this matter we discover that the wood the females gather for the hut (*imba*) is light, whereas that used for the *dare* consists of heavier logs and branches much easier for the men to chop and carry. The woman goes to the well or stream to fetch water for cooking, drinking or washing. She makes the clay pots but not other cooking utensils such as spoons or plates. Mats and baskets are made by men and they build the huts and granaries except the small granary called a *gombana* in which seed is kept.

A rough indication for determining whether a duty belongs to the man or woman is to note whether or not this responsibility is accompanied by any risk of injury. Carrying something heavy falls into this category; milking a cow involves a risk. Fishing is a male occupation although today women are sometimes seen at the side of a river with rods in their hands. A fishing net is heavy; also obviously there is the risk of attack by crocodiles or even, when alone at the water's edge, by strange men.

As well as the special duties for the two sexes, each member of a family knows his own place in it and there is a strict order of precedence in everything. There should be no misunderstanding as to what each has to do. For instance, when there is a ritual sacrifice, it is the duty of the son-in-law and his family to kill the beast. He has to skin it and remove certain parts of the carcass, even though it may be heavy and the task entail great effort. He also collects wood for the fire on which the pieces of meat are roasted before being offered to the family spirits. If he lives at his wife's village it is his task to prepare the fire at the *dare* every morning. He has to drink the first cup of beer at a beer ceremony.

This is often unappetizing, because of the cockroaches and other insects that fall into it when it is being prepared. When eating at the *dare* he sits apart from his father-in-law and his kinsmen and eats with the young sons and unmarried men. For a few weeks after he comes to the village as a newly-wed he is not permitted to eat at the *dare*, but must have his meals in one of the huts with his wife's sisters (*varamu*). We are puzzled by the fact that the son-in-law is called upon to perform what we consider menial duties, but this in no way signifies that he holds an inferior position in his society or that he can be trifled with—far from it; perhaps this is an instance of the joking relationship often found in African society and often revolving around the son-in-law.

Special ritual duties fall on the nephew (*muzukuru*), the eldest son of the eldest sister of the father. If he is absent, they are performed by the next eldest brother. At any religious ceremony he is the master of ceremonies and has to ensure the carrying out of the correct procedures. He assists in the different phases of the ceremony as the elder of the family group. He is also the go-between in all minor arguments. Any difference between members of the family should be brought to him and he reports it to the grandfather or father who is the head of the family. It is incorrect for the matter to be taken direct to the grandfather.

Matters relating to sex or others of a private or personal nature relating to the grown-up sons or daughters are dealt with by the aunt (sister of the father) *vatete*, and she may refer them to the parents. In strictly traditional society it is customary for the youngest daughter of the family and her husband to remain in the village when she marries instead of moving to her husband's home. She is in reality the *vatete*, but nowadays any of the father's sisters can assume the duty of the youngest aunt.

This method of referring problems to, or discussing certain matters with, the nephew or the youngest aunt on the father's side interests me greatly. My impression is that a man's sister and her children are likely to be less envious of their brother's children than would be those of blood brothers among whom relations may not always be as pleasant and satisfactory as they generally are between the brother and his sisters and their families.

THE MALE

From the time he starts to walk a boy quickly learns that he is not like his sisters and that he is more akin to his father. Although his mother still feeds him she never fails to let him know he is a boy and that his way of life is different from that of his sisters. His path soon diverges from theirs and by the time he is 5 or 6 years old he plays with or follows his older brothers and watches carefully what his father does.

His most important training takes place from about the age of 9, by which time he knows that he will never be called upon to cook his food; that his sisters are responsible for fetching water for the men of the family and that he does not go into the woods to gather wild fruit and vegetables for the household. Now, too, his training is taken over

A field of mhunga. (bulrush millet) (see page 8.)

A typical Shona field of maize in which pumpkins can also be seen growing. (see page 8.)

Winnowing in the Kandeya reserve, Mount Darwin district. (see page 22.)

Filling her basket as the woman proceeds to winnow the grain. (see page 22.)

by his father or grandfather. He also learns a good deal from his brothers and is admitted to the *dare* where the men of the village gather for their meals and discussions.

There are many important matters for him to learn, although today some of the duties normally undertaken by the male are no longer performed. For instance, there is no longer the need to learn to hunt, and even basket and mat-making are becoming obsolete. Instead he spends a good deal of his time at school. As a result many of the duties I am describing here as part of the traditional life of a village have now been discontinued because of European influence and so are carried out only in a few of the more remote parts of Mashonaland.

The father himself teaches his son how to make the handle (*mupini*) of a hoe or axe. He shows him which is the most suitable wood for this and takes him to the forest to choose a thin enough tree. He looks for one 3 or 4 feet high with three roots that branch out in different directions and then tells his son to dig round it and remove the soil, to expose the roots so that he can inspect them more closely to see if the main root will make a good head for his implement. If he is satisfied he chops the side roots through, digs deeper to see more of the main root and finally cuts through this so that the tree falls. He strips the bark of the pole that he has just cut and teaches the boy how to fashion the head with an adze (*mbezo*), and smooth its surface with a piece of metal that has a sharp end (*tsendo*). Finally he takes a piece of coal from the fire (*tsito* or *zimbe*) and marks the spot on the head where a hole is pierced with a thin wire called *muhururo*.

He also shows his son how to make a rope for trapping buck or a trap known as *dibu* (with a string and pole) for the same purpose. The boy is also taught how to make certain kitchen utensils for his mother, such as a big spoon (*mugwaku*), a plate (*ndiro*) and a basket (*tswanda*). He then learns from his father how to make a mat (*rukukwe*) from reeds called *tsanga*.

A boy of 9 is also taught how to prepare suitable firewood,

3

cutting it to the correct size, removing its bark and arranging it in bundles. He has to know the various types of firewood to be used for certain rituals. For example he must know the right kind to look for for his future father-in-law when he is about to be married. He must know that it is a man's duty to carry the thick heavier poles of firewood and stack them on the little platform (*bakwa*) just outside the door of the hut or even inside the hut itself. Each of these poles is about 4 to 6 feet long and about 4 inches in diameter. The bundle of wood (*svingo*) gathered by the women and piled at the foot of a tree is called *chowe*. From this the wife takes the little sticks and stores them on top of the larger pieces (*matanda*) already placed on the *bakwa* by the men. There is a *bakwa*, or ledge, inside the hut as well as next to its entrance. The family gather wood in the spring when there is generally little to do in the gardens and, of course, no rain. In the rainy season the woman uses the wood from the *bakwa* outside, but in the spring that gathered in the woods or from the piles under the trees can be utilized at once as it is dry. In wet weather wood from the outside *bakwa* is stored on the ledge inside and is replaced from the piles under the trees. At night only wood from inside is used as the woman is afraid to go out in the dark because of wild animals.

The fire in the hut is made by the woman, but that at the *dare* by a man who is permitted to take some embers from the hut to light his fire. But if his wife should need a light for her fire from the *dare* she may not fetch it herself and must ask one of the men to bring an ember from the *dare* and light her fire for her. When food is cooked in the field the fire is lit by the woman.

At the age of 9 a boy is taught by his father to trap rats (*kuteya mariva*) and catch birds (*shiri*). If the father is skilled in the art of forging he teaches his son this when he is 9 or 10. About this time the boy is taught special games such as *homa*, for which the players use sticks bent at one end, rather like golf clubs. The *homa* itself is a round wooden ball about the size of a tennis ball. The stick is called *tsvimbo yehoma*.

The game is played by four men or boys in an open place about 15 yards square with goals at opposite ends. The goal is simply a space between two stones. The ball is placed on the ground and two men stand outside each goal facing the opposite one for which they are aiming and they run and hit the ball, trying to drive it across the field into the appropriate goal, while their opponents try to stop them and drive it in the opposite direction. The principles are obviously the same as in our own more elaborate games of hockey or lacrosse, and not so very different from football.

Another game a father teaches his sons is called *nhindiri* and is also played by four people. Sticks about a yard long are cut with a sharp point at one end and each player holds two of these sticks, one in each hand. The bulbous root (*nhindiri*) is bowled into the middle by one of the players while the rest hurl their sticks at it, trying to pierce it as it moves slowly along the ground. If one of them succeeds he changes places with the bowler who joins the others and takes his turn at hurling the sticks.

THE ELDEST SON

Even today the eldest son is expected to remain in his parents' village when he marries. When he first brings his wife to the village they share the parents' *imba* in the daytime but sleep in his *gota* (subsidiary hut) at night. They help the parents in their gardens and store the grain in the same granary. Eventually—sometimes as much as five years later —the eldest son is allowed his own *imba*, which he and his father erect together. The *vatete* (sister of his father) or the grandmother, if there is no aunt, procures the cooking utensils for his wife. These comprise:

1. A clay cooking-pot called *tsaiya*.
2. A pot for meat and relish (*hadyana*).
3. A basket (*tswanda*).
4. Two cooking sticks for stirring (*migoti*).
5. A special stick used as a whisk (*musika*).
6. A hoe (*badza*).

7. A wooden plate (*ndiro*).
8. A small clay pot in which to serve relish to the men (*chimbiya*).

The grandfather (*sekuru*) gives his grandson an axe (*demo*), a bow (*huta*) and two arrows (*miseve*) and the father gives him a field and some oxen for ploughing.

The eldest son (*dangwe*) succeeds his father as head of the family and thus is second to his father in the village if there are no brothers of his father. He works for his parents, tends their gardens as well as his own, assists with the cattle and with the building and repairing of the cattle-pen and the living-huts, and shares with his brothers and brothers-in-law the task of cutting and bringing the large, heavy firewood to the village.

THE YOUNGER BROTHER

The duties of the younger sons are similar to those of their eldest brother. When a younger son marries and brings his wife to live in his father's village, he informs his eldest brother that he is living in his own hut with his wife. If he upsets the ancestral spirits *(vadzimu)* in any way or if, at a later date, he wishes to leave the village he must tell the eldest brother, who passes on the information to the father. If he decides to settle elsewhere, his eldest brother should accompany him to his new place of abode and help him build a hut and prepare new fields.

DUTIES OF A GIRL

A girl, like her brother, soon discovers that certain tasks have to be carried out only by members of her sex. Her mother is careful to indoctrinate her from about the age of 4 with what is expected of a woman. All her instruction is aimed at preparing her for the ultimate object of marriage, and her training is continued until she is about 17 or 18 when it is confidently expected that she will marry a good and suitable man.

From childhood onwards, therefore, the girl is in close contact with her mother, her sisters and her other female relations in the village. A good deal of her time is devoted to learning to cook, prepare food and collect firewood and fetch water. From about 5 or 6 years a little girl is encouraged to play in the sand outside the hut with a few pieces of broken plates or pots or, nowadays, even jam-tins with which she pretends to cook just like her mother. She pretends the sand is meal and makes 'cereal porridge' out of it. As she becomes older the game becomes more real. First she may be given a lighted ember to place under the pot, which she has learnt to rest on stones. During the game she shows her cooking to her mother and asks her advice and the mother enters into the game with all seriousness and even pretends to taste the finished product. This pretence goes on for three or four years until the mother feels the girl is old enough and sufficiently capable of helping her with the actual preparation and cooking of food in the hut.

From about the age of 7 she is taught to grind the millet or other cereals into meal, and how to prepare the ground-nuts so often used for making relish. She is shown how to make the stiff porridge (*sadza*) and by the age of 9 can be trusted to watch over it while it is cooking on the fire. If by any chance her mother is called away from home, she can be trusted to cook it on her own. She soon learns that her father must be served first and his portion of porridge placed on his own special plate.

From about 7 or 8 a girl is shown how to use a hoe for weeding instead of the small one she was given earlier. She is taught the proper way to hoe a field and to weed (*kusakura*) it with a small hoe (*kaserima*). From about 10 she learns how to sow seeds in the fields and how to spread the finger millet and ground-nuts to dry. She must know how to cut grass for thatching although the thatching itself is done by the male.

Her mother takes her into the bush and shows her the best kind of wood to gather for the fire. Every girl must know all about the preparation of beer and she starts learning this art from her mother when she is about 15 years old.

Explanation of menstruation may be an embarrassment to the mother so all explanations of such delicate matters related to sex are the duty of the *vatete*—the girl's youngest aunt on her father's side, who plays a special role in the lives of her nieces and nephews. When she starts to menstruate the girl goes to this aunt and if her mother discovers it first she sends her to her. As she is now likely to be married in five or six years' time this aunt now tells her all about sex, explaining solemnly and quietly what happens. She tells her about the sanctity of marriage and warns her not to become too friendly with boys. She is told all about the marriage relationship and of her duty to please her husband. She also learns from the *vatete* the significance of pregnancy and what procedures are to be adopted when she falls pregnant or if she fails to conceive, in which case she must inform her parents so that she can be seen by a good *nganga* and receive the necessary medicines. From now onwards the girl is subjected to a regular inspection of her genitalia by her grandmother or one of her father's sisters to ensure that she remains a virgin until she is married. Virginity is highly prized, and in Shona society penalties can be exacted if a bride is not a virgin. The girl is generally taken to a secluded spot near a river and lies down on a reed mat while she is inspected. In some places this is done at regular intervals, but in others only when it is suspected that she is becoming too friendly with boys. The inspection is called *mwana aiswa mashambo*. It is hardly ever carried out nowadays, but I have met parents who told me their daughters were still inspected. Others regret that the practice is being discontinued because of European influence, and in consequence they consider the dignity and status of the woman are being lost.

When a girl is about to be married, during the brideprice *(roora)* proceedings, she is again inspected, usually a week after the bridewealth has been paid—but often the day before she leaves for her husband's home. If she is a virgin her father asks for a payment called *mombe yechishava* from her husband's family. This is paid later when the ritual of *masungiro* is performed. The ox that is paid is a sign that the girl was a virgin when she married. But before it is handed over, the go-between brings a small piece of cloth, called *mundya*, from the son-in-law, and without making his presence known, places it at the door of the father-in-law's house. This is done after the bride has slept with her husband. It is believed that if the ceremony of *masungiro* is not carried out, all those concerned will suffer from backache.

The importance of the family unit is stressed from an early age. The Shona realizes that the boy and girl must grow up well trained and be ready to accept the responsibilities of marriage. Each boy and girl must know what is expected of them and how to perform their duties in a practical way. Therefore they have an interesting practice called *mahumbwe* which can best be described as a trial marriage but without sexual intimacy. The home life of a Shona married man and woman is enacted by each couple under the parents' vigilance. From the ages of 10 or 11 the boys and girls of the village are paired off, the boy taking the part of the husband and the girl that of the wife. One or two toddlers may even be given to them for children. There are a variable number of couples and this event takes place towards the end of harvest time, when a little *rukweza* and other crops are purposely left in the fields for the young couples to gather. The little husband builds a hut or, more simply, constructs a circular shelter or even a depression in the ground to represent the hut. These are built a little distance from the village and at night the children return to their parents to sleep. In the daytime during the two or three weeks that *mahumbwe* lasts, the boys reap the crops and go out in small groups to snare small animals or trap birds and mice. They bring back their kill to their 'wives' who cook the meals and bring the food to their 'husbands' at the *dare*, in the same way as their parents. The following year the ceremony is repeated by all the children of this age group and often the same couples act as husband and wife. *Mahumbwe* still takes place today in some of the rural districts although with the spread of European culture it is rapidly disappearing.

INITIATION RITES

Among Bantu tribes other than the Shona initiation rites are generally practised to a greater or lesser extent, so, although they do not occur among the Shona, they are worth a brief reference.

Simmons (1960)[1] describes the operation of *clitoridectomy* carried out on the girls of the Efik people of Calabar, Nigeria. This was usually performed between the ages of 9 and 11 when the girl was placed in a house of 'seclusion' where a woman specialist excised her hymen and the upper external cuticle of the clitoris with a straight razor. Then she was kept in seclusion from two to seven years while she was instructed in the art of preparing food and the correct behaviour of a woman towards her husband. Ideally a girl in seclusion never indulged in sexual intercourse with her intended husband.

Boys among the Efik were circumcised by women specialists.

Culwick,[2] too, refers to the not uncommon custom of secluding young girls at puberty for a period varying from the duration of the first menstrual cycle to a matter of months or even years. In the first case she was merely removed from normal social contact during a short period of crisis, when certain rites had to be performed for her own safety and fertility and instructions as to her personal conduct were driven home. Strict separation of the sexes is practised; no girl is allowed to mix freely with boys until she has reached an age when she may think of marriage. Sexual relations are strictly forbidden and only permitted after the rather lengthy marriage formalities have been completed. Boys and girls can take part together in various procedures

[1] Simmons, D. C. *Africa* (1960), *30*, 153.
[2] Culwick, G. M. *Africa* (1939), *12*, 425.

that are carried out in the village but nothing of an intimate nature is allowed. 'Mosa' is a special term used to denote that a boy and girl have become sexually involved.

In Mashonaland children are warned that they dare not eat meals other than those prepared in their own *imba*. They are not permitted to go to their mothers for a second meal and they are told that if they do this they will develop a second umbilicus (*makuvu maviri*), so they are afraid to break the rules.

THE DUTIES OF A WIFE

A wife's duties are clearly defined and may be listed as follows:

1. To look after her husband and especially to provide his meals.
2. To look after the children.
3. To see that the huts are kept clean and tidy by sweeping the floors and smearing them with cow dung at regular intervals, usually once or twice a week.
4. To collect firewood for the fire in the hut and grass for thatching the roof.
5. To fetch water for cooking and brewing beer.
6. To plant seed in the fields (also done by her husband).
7. To grind or stamp the various cereals into meal and to store the crops.

A man never plants ground-nuts or monkey-nuts, or sweet potatoes as they are considered female crops. There is a curious association between the planting of nuts and the menstrual cycle. In the Chikwaka reserve, for instance, a menstruating woman is permitted to sow the seeds, but once their shoots have appeared above the ground when she is menstruating she may only go into her own field of ground-nuts if she has not planted it herself. The same applies to rice. A woman who is menstruating is considered a danger to others and she should never visit a sick person lest the illness becomes worse. A pregnant woman is regarded in the same light, but she may care for a sick child. She can shake hands with healthy people. No doubt the taboos associated with menstruation and pregnancy vary from place to place.

The preparation of food in the *imba* must be done according to certain rules. A woman should never stand when she is cooking *sadza*; she must sit. In the evening or when it is dark a girl or even a young boy holds a lighted stick so that he can watch her cooking. If another adult woman is present in the *imba*, before she begins she must clap her hands. Then she says, '*Tibike*' (I am going to cook). She then washes her hands and sits down on the floor to cook.

When the *sadza* is ready she dishes it out into the various plates, one for her husband at the *dare*, one for herself, a third for her daughters and a fourth for the young sons. When this is done she claps her hands and says '*Tibure*' (we are going to take the *tsaya* from the fireplace). These two expressions are used as a sign of respect for the older or more senior women who are with her in the *imba*. A daughter cooking for her mother does not clap and say these words, but merely turns the pot towards her mother.

Before starting their meal the woman and her children all wash their hands and then sit cross-legged in a circle round the plates of *sadza*. The grown-up daughters share a plate and the youngest children eat from their mother's. The mother claps her hands and takes a small piece of *sadza* (*musuva*) to eat. Then the eldest girl claps hands and takes her first piece. Each one does likewise in order of seniority. They eat until they are satisfied. No child is permitted to receive any *sadza* without first clapping hands and no matter how young she is not given any food until she has complied. Children under 8, boys or girls, are not permitted to take a piece of *sadza* from the plate, but must wait until the mother hands over a piece. Young nieces or nephews eating with their aunt are given a separate plate. She takes this plate and divides the food into small portions which the little nephews and nieces are allowed to take for themselves, but she must hand her own little sons their portions from her plate. When the meal is finished they all wash their hands again and the eldest daughter collects the plates and washes them. If she has no daughter the mother takes away and washes the plates herself. When the men at the *dare* have eaten, the small boys who are old enough to eat there must bring dirty plates to their mother in the *imba*.

THE MUROORA
(The newly wedded wife)

When a bride first comes to live in the father-in-law's village she is taken to the aunt (*vatete*) who presents her with a gift so that she can enter her hut. If there is no aunt in the village this ceremonial is performed by the grandmother. The new arrival then eats food with the aunt and her husband's sisters. Again before she consents to eat she is given another present. All, except the *vatete*, who has hers on a separate plate, share from the same plate no matter what age they are. The *muroora* eats only a small amount and on this particular occasion, as a special privilege, may finish before the sisters-in-law. Normally after a meal the *muroora* is expected to remove the dirty plates for washing, but for this particular one it is done by one of her husband's sisters.

The morning after her arrival the newly-wed woman has a special duty to perform. She rises early, fetches water, warms it and then goes round to each of the men, giving him some water with which to wash his face. In return he presents her with a bangle (*ndarira*). A more important man, such as the chief, offers her a fowl.

The same day the aunt takes her to her mother-in-law's *imba*, but before she enters the aunt has to give her a small gift from her mother-in-law and sisters-in-law else she refuses to go inside. Once in the hut she sits on the mat with her legs stretched straight in front of her, but crossed at the ankles with her neck well bent and her eyes on the ground. Again the aunt gives her a present and tells her that she must know it is her duty to clean this hut and that she should not

be afraid of any kind of work in it. 'This is your *imba* in which
to work.'

From now onwards she works in her mother-in-law's
hut, cooks the food for the family, stamps grain, prepares
the ground monkey-nut relish called *dovi* and helps collect
water and wood. She also has to smear the floor of the hut
with dung at regular intervals. In the Chikwaka reserve this
must be done for the first time within a week of her arrival
and, on this occasion, before she begins she stands outside
the entrance until her mother-in-law presents her with a
bangle as a mark of appreciation for the trouble she is taking.

She works in her mother-in-law's hut for some time, perhaps a year or two or even three or five, but nowadays it is
generally much less. If she bears a child in the meantime she
may continue to help her mother-in-law for even longer
instead of housekeeping for herself. She sleeps in a separate
hut with her husband, but eats from the same plate as her
mother-in-law and sisters-in-law. She must always respect
his sisters, even if they are younger than she and must always
wait until they have had their first morsels of food before
taking hers. Although she is permitted to dip her piece of
solid porridge in the relish she may not take any meat from
the pot (*hadyana*). Her mother-in-law hands her a piece.

When her father-in-law thinks the time has come for his
son to have his own *imba*, he selects a site for it, marks the
spot with a line or simply a hole in the ground and instructs
the young man to commence building his home there.
When it is ready for occupation the aunt obtains the necessary
cooking utensils for the young wife and in her presence
prepares stiff porridge in the new hut and shows her which
is her husband's plate and which is her own. When the meal
is prepared the aunt formally conducts the young couple to
the hut and shows the wife her fireplace. She says, 'This is
your own house, in which you will live and take charge of
your own affairs'. If there is no aunt, the grandmother performs this ceremony. From now onwards the young wife
cooks her husband's *sadza* and takes it to him at the *dare*.
But she still does not eat alone in her hut. She takes her plate

of food to her mother-in-law's *imba* and the two women eat together from the same plate. This goes on for a long time, perhaps even six years, by which time she may have two or three children of her own. Then at last the mother-in-law decides that she and her children should eat in their own hut. The first-born, however, usually remains with the grandparents; although one of the other children may be chosen instead as they usually prefer a girl.

When a visitor arrives in the village it is the duty of the *muroora* to take him a plate of porridge. She cooks for the visitor and serves him when the family are busy in the fields. When a beast (*mombe*) sheep or goat is killed the *muroora* cleans the intestines and prepares the liver and lungs for cooking and in return it is customary for the father to present her with the hind leg of any animal killed. When the meat is cooked she is not permitted to serve it as this is the duty of her mother-in-law. But she serves the *sadza*. She prepares the fermented grain (*mamera*) when her mother-in-law brews beer and also fetches the water for it.

If there is more than one newly wedded wife in the village the mother-in-law (*vamwene*) decides which task each should perform and if the *muroora's* husband takes a second wife she serves the mother-in-law in the *imba* in the same way as the first wife did.

THE VAHOSI (FIRST WIFE)

When a man has more than one wife the first or chief wife is known as the *vahosi*. She is the important woman in the family and ultimately responsible for the well-being of the whole family including the children of the other wife or wives. She has the authority to chide any of the others if she misbehaves or does something that does not meet with the approval of the society in which she lives. If this woman takes no notice of her injunctions she has the right to report her to their husband. The *vahosi*, or her deputy, brings the food to the husband's *dare*. When he returns from a hunting expedition with game he divides it among the wives, but this is done in the hut of the *vahosi*.

The responsibility of feeding the husband rests with the *vahosi*, who is assisted by the others according to her instructions. Each wife cooks in her own *imba* and what she sends to the *dare* depends on the wishes of the *vahosi*. The latter may depute any of the other wives to provide food for the husband on certain days of the week. Each wife eats in her own *imba* except when she first arrives, when, for a time, she works and eats in the hut of the mother-in-law (*vamwene*).

When beer is to be brewed the husband tells one of the wives when he wants it and she asks the *vahosi* or the other wife to lend a hand.

The second wife (*mukaranga*) and third wife (*murongo*) are given their own portions of land to plough, but the first wife is the one who is entitled to enter the husband's fields to gather the ripe grain and when his land is to be weeded he instructs her to do so. She passes word round to the others and they all weed the husband's field. *Zunde* is the husband's field and all the family are obliged to weed it before working in their own, and the husband decides which of his fields should be done first. He is not obliged to plough or weed his wives' land, but may help them if he wishes.

When the fields are to be planted the husband takes seed (*mbeu*) from his granary, gives some to the first wife and then to each of the others in order of precedence and they all go out together to plant it—first in his lands, of course, then in that of the first wife and then in the others, but all working together in each.

In March (*Kurume*) when the mealies are ripe, before they can be eaten, the first wife takes two cobs from her husband's land, roasts them and gives one to her youngest child and one to the second wife's. She then takes two more from his lands and places them on a dried tree stump (*gutsa*) saying, 'Crows (*makunguo*), here are your mealies, keep away from our gardens'. But the family spirits or *vadzimu* must also be remembered so she takes six more cobs from the same garden and places them at the foot of a *muhacha* tree, kneels under it and claps her hands praying, 'Look after the mealies in the lands so that crows do not come in. Help us to eat mealies in the village without any sickness.' Next to the mealies she places a plate of *mumera* made up of meal (*upfu*) ground from the sprouted seed of some other grain such as *mhunga*, *mapfunde* or *rukweza*, but not of maize. After the prayers have been said the small children fill their hands with the *mumera* and rub it over one another's faces. Now the *vahosi* is permitted to pick cobs from her husband's lands whenever she wishes. The second wife is not allowed to pick cobs from his lands without first seeking permission from the *vahosi*. Of course the second wife needs no permission to pick from her own lands.

After the spirits have received their share and the husband's grain has been dried on a rock (*ruware*) the exact amount of each kind is measured in a large basket (*dengu*). Each wife is given one basketful of each variety from his stock and the rest is stored in his granary. Then the wives' crops are measured in the same way in order of seniority before being stored in their own granaries. Each wife uses her own store of grain first and when this is finished is permitted to use the husband's. But this is shared out by the first wife.

THE ADDITIONAL WIVES (CO-WIVES)

There are a number of reasons for a man to want an extra wife. It is not merely because of his desire for a younger woman to satisfy his sexual needs, but more often due to the wish of both husband and wife for extra help in the home, village and lands. Not infrequently when a wife begins to age and is finding it a hardship to work in the fields as well as perform her other duties, she may suggest to her husband that it would be a good idea to find a younger wife to join them in the village. Further, the first wife may even choose the second one, but more often she leaves this to her husband. Nevertheless a husband is expected to obtain his wife's permission and her approval of his choice before he marries again. Usually he brings a second wife into the village only if his wife is happy about it. But this is not always the case; sometimes he ignores her opposition.

The second wife is given her own hut in which to sleep and takes over the task of carrying her husband's cooked food to the *dare*. She spends her days with the first wife in the main *imba* for about a month until the *vahosi* feels she is acquainted with all that goes on in the village. She then presents her with her own hearth-stones (*mapfihwa*) for her hut, where she now cooks. She takes the food she has cooked for her husband to the *dare* and then takes a plate of food to the *vahosi's* hut, where the two women share it, eating from the same plate. Her duties depend mainly on what the *vahosi* requires of her. She must obey her instructions. When visitors come to the village the second wife is usually deputed to look after them—prepare sleeping-quarters for them and cook for them. If beer has to be brewed for any occasion the second wife brews it under the direction of the *vahosi*. When it is ready she has to inform the first wife.

THE DUTIES OF THE MUZUKURU

A *muzukuru* is a son or daughter of the sister of the father of a family or of his own or his brother's sons. The sisters' children are known as *vazukuru* and the brothers' children as *vanakomana* (sons) and *vanasikana* (daughters) because they are of the same blood as their uncle. If the eldest child of the father's son is also a boy he is sent at about the age of 8 to live with his grandfather and grandmother. He is given his own hut (*gota*) in which to sleep, but although his parents are in the same village, he spends his time with the grandparents. He accompanies his grandfather when he goes hunting to carry his weapons and his food in a special fibre bag called *nhava*. He helps him with his hunting, skins the animals he kills and takes the portions of meat to the various members of the family as directed by his grandfather. As mentioned earlier, the *muzukuru* acts as master of ceremonies at all religious ceremonies but does not say the prayers as this is done by the head man of the family.

If the eldest son's eldest child is a girl she is sent at about the age of 10 to help her grandparents. She lives with them,

A typical wooden structure used for storing dry grass required for thatching. (Chikwaka reserve, central Mashonaland.) (see page 22.)

A father and son at the plough in the Nyandoro reserve. (see page 22.)

The cattle kraal or *dhanga*—a very familiar site in every Shona village. (see page 22.)

Cattle grazing in the Nyandoro reserve. (see page 22.)

fetches their water and firewood and sweeps their hut. When the grandmother is ill she gives her her medicines, usually in her porridge. She helps in the grandparents' garden and, when she is old enough, assists her grandmother with the brewing of beer. Even if one of the grandparents is dead this little girl is still sent to help the surviving one. When she marries, her grandparents are presented with a beast (*mombe*) —an ox or cow called *chiredzwa*—as an expression of gratitude to them. If there are no grandchildren the son's wife (*muroora*) performs the duties of the female *muzukuru* and the daughter's husband (*mukuwasha*) those of the male *muzukuru*.

After a man's death it is the duty of his *muzukuru* (sister's senior son) to divide the clothes and other belongings of the deceased among his family. The *muzukuru* also conducts the ceremony of handing over the widow to one of her late husband's brothers. Apart from those of the master of ceremonies he has no special duties in the burial ceremony but on other ritual occasions among his other duties he has to share out the pots of beer.

A *muzukuru* has the privilege of being able to eat whatever he fancies in his *sekuru's* home and no one is permitted to complain about any of his actions.

A male *muzukuru* living with the grandparents fetches water, collects firewood and cleans the hut for them, but he does not help with the cooking. If the grandmother is too old to cook, the boy's mother does it on his behalf and he carries the food to the old people. When a female *muzukuru* marries, if there is no other girl to look after the grandparents she may take them with her to her husband's village.

THE AUNT (VATETE)

The term *vatete* used for the aunt refers only to the sisters of the father of a family. In strictly traditional society, when a girl marries she moves to her husband's village, but the youngest daughter of the family is required to remain with her husband in her father's village and because of this the amount of bridewealth paid by her husband is lowered. This aunt remains in the village because she has special duties to perform. She advises her brothers' children on sex matters and on anything appertaining to marriage. It is incorrect for his children to approach their father directly about any important request or issue to be decided. They must first see their *vatete*, who discusses the question with their father.

Nowadays this duty may be performed by any of the father's sisters, particularly by the eldest sister. If she is living in the village or near by she is the one to be approached if the children have a request and she also instructs them on matters of sex and marriage and welcomes her nephew's bride to her hut when it is ready. Moreover her eldest son, or even one of her other children, is known as the *muzukuru* and is required to settle minor quarrels in the village or even to restore peace in an argument between his uncle and his wife.

THE DUTIES OF THE OLD WOMEN

Broadly speaking there are two kinds of elderly women in a village. First, there are those who are so old they cannot do anything for themselves and require grandchildren to care for them. Then there are the old women who are still fit enough to undertake some useful tasks. They tend their own small gardens, although they are not able to put in the same effort as younger people. They do a little weeding, as every extra hand is useful and help look after the grandchildren, particularly the babies, while the mothers attend to other duties. In their own little gardens they grow monkey-nuts and cow peas, which are easier to handle than grain, which requires more attention. The younger women of the village help them with the planting and weeding as, except for the son-in-law, men are not permitted to work with these female crops. Often the old people's fields are tended before the others, except of course those of the headman of the village. The men, however, keep an eye on the old women's fields and drive away any wild animals that might be a danger to the crops. Each old woman keeps a supply of seeds in her own hut ready to plant the next rainy season. When her crops are ready she gives her grandchildren the first monkey-nuts to taste. They are eaten raw. If she has grown mealies the grandchildren also eat the first fruits which are roasted for them.

The grandfather also has his garden if he is well enough to work in it, and is helped in the same way by the men of the village. The grandfather and grandmother share a grain bin (*dura*) to store their crops.

MUGARIRI

If a father wishes his daughter to live in his village when she marries he forgoes some of the *roora* that he would normally receive, as compensation to the son-in-law for moving to her village. This generally happens when the daughter is the youngest (*gotwe*) girl in the family and thus she is the aunt or *vatete* to her brothers' children. Sometimes too a father permits his daughter to marry a poor man who has no bridewealth (*roora*) to pay for her. In this case the husband is known as *mugarari*, and when he marries the girl his father-in-law reminds him that he must obey his orders and must never be lazy or cruel to his wife. *Masungiro* is still performed after the marriage, and the go-between acts in the same way as if *roora* had been paid. The father-in-law provides a hut for the young people and gives his son-in-law a field, but the young man builds his own store-room (*hozi*) for his crops. When he has been given his hut the son-in-law informs the villagers that he has his own home and his friends and well-wishers present him with the utensils needed in it. The son-in-law who cannot afford to pay *roora* lives and works in his father-in-law's village until he can pay his debt.

Another person referred to as *mugariri* is the indigent man who attaches himself to, and works for, some other person in the village, thus corresponding to what used to be known as a domestic slave. Later this man may marry one of his master's daughters and would have to pay a small *roora* perhaps only a hoe. But his wife would remain in her father's village and the children of the marriage belong to her father until the *roora* is paid. The verb *Kugarira* means to wait for. This form of marriage is probably very uncommon nowadays. Most sons-in-law prefer to pay *roora* and can earn money in one of the towns for this purpose.[3]

MORALS

Throughout Mashonaland, if a baby or small child becomes ill, suspicion may fall upon its mother. Its illness is often attributed to a bad deed on the mother's part, and particularly if her husband is away working in a town when the child becomes sick, she is suspected of having committed adultery. Further it is believed that it will not recover and may even die if the mother does not confess her guilt. As children often become ill and many husbands are away in the towns, the wife is often suspect. The fear that she might lose a child through having illicit relations with a lover in her husband's absence is often a deterrent to a woman who might otherwise be tempted and in this way the sanctity of marriage is often preserved. If a woman has an obstructed labour, the same suspicions are aroused and she is asked to confess if she has a secret lover, so that the baby may be delivered without further trouble.

Margaret Read's description of the strict moral code among the Ngoni, an offshoot of the Zulu, has much in common with that of the Shona. According to her it aims at controlling the physical and emotional sexual impulses in individuals. The brideprice was high, but if a girl was found to have had sexual intercourse before marriage she was in disgrace and a smaller *roora* was paid to her father. Read also mentioned that periodic inspection of the girls was carried out by the older women after they reached puberty. When the first menstrual cycle took place, the girl was kept at home and afterwards was taken to a river to bathe. Here she received careful instruction about correct conduct and

[3] Chigumi. *Native Affairs Department Annual* (1923), 79.

clothing and was told never to expose her private parts. When she was preparing for her marriage there was a special ritual ceremony called *umsindo* which could be held only if, on examination, the girl proved to be a virgin. Read points out from the commencement of her menses for a period of ten or fifteen years the girl had to be particularly careful to keep flirting within bounds. As a result divorce was unusual among the Ngoni and adultery even rarer.

The sanctity of the institution had to be maintained after marriage. Death was the penalty for adultery. Fidelity in marriage had two main sanctions. The first was its effect on the woman's labour in childbirth. Then there were two special illnesses that raised suspicions of adultery. The first was called *insila* and caused a man to have a black look on his face as well as pains in his limbs. The second was *ugola*, a wasting disease caused by a medicine given to his wife by a suspicious husband, so that her guilty lover would waste away.[4]

[4] Read, M. *Africa* (1938), *11*, 1.

5   *Friendship in Shona Society*

In the family the Shona has a set mode of behaviour but, even in times that the European considers highly informal the Shona has his predetermined social code. Has the term friend the same meaning to the Shona as it has to the European? Has he friends comparable to those seen in European society? The African living in urban areas, removed from his traditional environment, has, to a certain extent, adopted European modes of behaviour and can consider his friendships similar to those existing in European society. There different classes of Africans meet and so many friendships develop through common interests.

What do we mean by friendship in a European society? I venture to describe it as an association built up by men or women with others outside their family circle. It is determined by many factors, such as similar religious beliefs, common language, school or place of origin, the same nationality or similar interests. Usually this relationship is a loose one; it is subject to change and is not often relied upon in times of crisis or tragedy. But many people in European society find one or more true friends who help them when the occasion arises and in whom they can place their trust as with their own family.

THE SHAMWARI

The Shona, too, enjoys a circle of friends, but most of them live in their own or near-by villages and are thus members of their wide family circle. This larger family circle is composed of two groups—the *vazukuru* or blood relations and the *vakuwasha* or relations by marriage of the family. Be-

46

tween the people of near-by villages a friendly understanding springs up over the years, especially among those with the same totem and *chidao*, for they are really part of a large tribal family protected by the same *mhondoro* (tribal spirit) and originally stem from the same parent or founder of the tribe. Such a friend is called a *shamwari*.

The term *shamwari* refers to an ordinary friendship existing between people and can best be described perhaps as an acquaintanceship. Among the Vakaranga (the Shona who mostly live around Fort Victoria) the corresponding word is *Hama* (friendly neighbour or relative), but when they speak of *shamwari* they would be referring to one who is called *sahwira* elsewhere. Another variety of friendship is embodied in the term *munyai*, of which there are two kinds. The first, also called *dombo*, is the go-between in the marriage ritual, the man selected by the *mukuwasha* (the son-in-law or, at this stage, the man who wishes to marry a certain girl) and sent to the *tezvara* (father-in-law or rather, at this stage, the girl's father) to arrange the marriage. The *munyai* is usually married himself and may be a relative (*muzukuru*) or even a *shamwari*. The other kind of *munyai*, also known as *muranda*, is one who needs a home and is permitted by the village head to live in his village. Living in the midst of a family as he does, he soon comes to be no longer regarded as a stranger by the rest of the villagers and in fact is quickly looked upon as 'part of the family' and more than likely marries a daughter of the village head.

THE CUSTOM OF HOKA OR NHIMBE

Friendship or friendliness between groups of villagers— men and women from different but neighbouring villages— is strikingly demonstrated by the custom of *nhimbe* or *hoka*, which is practised at certain times of the year when weeding has to be done or the crops harvested. All surrounding friends and relations are invited to the village of the person whose field is to be weeded, ploughed or reaped. They all come for the day and help to complete the appointed task.

Pots of beer are produced during the day and the occasion is a happy one. This custom is an essential part of the life of the Shona and shows his desire to be on friendly terms with his neighbours and to share their work and pleasures with them.

In the Chikwaka district, for example, when a man needs help in his fields his wife prepares beer and then informs the *sabuku* (headman) that he intends holding a *hoka* and will be inviting his friends and relatives to the village. On the appointed day the men arrive with their wives and children at about eight in the morning. After ploughing for two or three hours, they outspan their oxen and rest for a few hours, commencing work again when it is a little cooler. During this break they drink the beer and eat the meat provided by the man who has asked for their help. Later at about five in the evening a last pot of beer, known as *mharadzo*, is produced as a signal for the workers to disperse. *Hoka* is held in November for ploughing, in January for weeding (*kusakura*) and in April or May for harvesting (*kukohwa*). A separate *hoka* is arranged for each of his fields by the farmer who owns much land, provided, of course, he can spare sufficient millet *(rukweza)* for the beer. *Hoka* is considered proper for a *hurudza* or big farmer who must prepare the beer with which to reward his neighbours for performing specific tasks in his lands, but it is a purely voluntary affair and no one is obliged to hold this ceremony unless he wishes. The small farmer with too little *rukweza* for beer relies on *jangano*, whereby his friends and relatives help him with his ploughing without being recompensed with beer.

USAHWIRA

It is difficult to know how often true friendship exists in European society. By this I mean a friendship which carries. with it a deep understanding between two people who place utmost trust in one another and can depend on each other in times of trouble. It would be fair to say that such friendship is well known, but certainly uncommon. In African society friendship with outsiders or strangers is likely to be restricted because of the risk of forming an association with someone who may possess the traits of a witch. This is a real fear which to some extent limits the development of friendships outside the family circle. Yet as if to make up for this reluctance to make friends with strangers there is a special friendship not usually seen in European society. In contrast to the *shamwari* or friendly acquaintance to whom I have already referred as being so frequent in both African and European society, there is the *sahwira* who is the true, trusted and lifelong friend of a man or a woman. Every married man and probably every married woman among the Shona should have a *sahwira* or ritual friend who is of the same sex but of a different totem. This friendship must be established and accepted by both parties as lifelong and unbreakable.

The friendship *usahwira*, as it is called, is first celebrated among the Shona with the preparation of beer by one of the ritual friends and shortly after this by a ceremony with meat. Each friend becomes known as a *sahwira*. Usually a person chooses for his *sahwira* someone with the same interests as himself and whose temperament does not clash with his own. A quiet, steady man looks for a *sahwira* with similar qualities and one who drinks excessively chooses one with the same habits as himself. A man with agricultural interests selects a friend who has similar tastes, while a hunter chooses one following the same pursuit as he.

Frequently a *sahwira* friendship starts at a beer party where two people previously not much acquainted with one another strike up a friendship. When an understanding has been established and strengthened by subsequent meetings one of the parties makes the first move by having beer brewed for his friend, whom he invites to a party. If the latter wishes to accept the friendship *(usahwira)*, he attends the beer ceremony and then reciprocates by holding another party at which meat is provided for the one who brewed the beer.

The *sahwira* has two duties. After his friend's death he has to carry the body to its burial place and receive it inside the grave. The same applies to women except that the woman does not receive the body in the grave; instead on the day of the funeral she helps cook the food and meat for the mourners, leaving her husband to deputize for her in the grave. A *sahwira* has also to visit his friend when he is ill to see how he is progressing.

The friendship once established by two people may be continued by their children into the third or fourth generation. In this case there is no need for special parties to be held as this was done by their forebears. But it is not compulsory for the children to continue this friendship as they are at liberty to form their own friendships outside the two families. The *sahwira* is on a much more intimate footing than the *shamwari*, who is like any other acquaintance and is not permitted to enter his friend's house, nor is he taken into confidence or permitted to talk to him whenever he wishes or to occupy a position of importance at his *dare* (the special place in the village where the men have their meals); these are reserved for the *sahwira*, the true friend.

A person never gets angry with his *sahwira* even if hard words are used by the other or his errors pointed out to him. Even if called a *muroyi* (witch) he must contain himself. Even if he scolds one of his *sahwira's* relations or accuses him or the relation of witchcraft this accusation cannot be taken to the *dare* (the court where cases are heard). This applies to women as well as to men.

If a *sahwira* jokingly accuses his friend of being a *muroyi*, the latter can retaliate by taking one of his *sahwira's* goats, killing it and sharing the meat with his family and neighbours. The *sahwira* in turn goes to his friend's home, kills one or two of his fowls and takes them with him. But in spite of this they remain friends.

The ceremony establishing the *sahwira* friendship is a very important one, and though it is basically the same throughout Mashonaland it varies in detail from district to district. In Chikwaka's area I am told the *sahwira* is generally married by the time he enters into this arrangement. He need not be married, but he must be an adult. The first approaches often take place at harvest time during a *hoka* ceremony when one of the parties carefully collects a head (*hura*) of finger millet with the grains still on it. He gives this to the man he wishes to become his *sahwira*. The one who receives the head of grain counts the fingers (*mhaswa*) of grain on the head (there are three or four on each head) and his wife brews beer according to their number. The beer is carried to the village of the man who gave the grain. Stiff porridge (*sadza*) is cooked and a fowl killed for meat. They eat the porridge and drink a pot of beer, and then the visitors return to their own village, leaving the rest of the beer behind. The man who was given the beer now shares it with his relations and tells them that he has a *sahwira*. His relations present him with bangles (*ndarira*) or a *mukosi* (string of beads) to be worn round his waist, according to the number of pots of beer brought to the village. The wife of the *sahwira* washes the empty pots and returns them to the man who sent the beer together with a *ndarira* or *mukusu* for each pot of beer.

It is now the turn of the other *sahwira* to make beer, and when it is ready he invites his friend to come with his relations to his village. He kills a goat for them and they all eat stiff porridge and meat and drink beer, dance and are happy. As the party continues the two *sahwira* may smear mud or ash on each other or splash one another with water. Towards the end of the celebration one big pot of beer is produced and the *sahwira's* nephew proclaims, 'This is your big pool in which you are going to wash as you have been smearing *daka* or *dota* [earth, ashes] on me'. When this large pot of beer is finished they return to their homes. The next day three or four people return to the scene of the party and declare they are thirsty. They are given a pot of beer.

Three or four days later the other *sahwira* presents his friend with a beast (*mombe yousahwira*) in return for the beer party. This is accepted, and in order to thank his friend for the ox, the first *sahwira* prepares more beer. The two friends drink this with their families and friends. At a later date when the *sahwira* kills this *mombe* he sends the back and tail of the animal to his friend. Each time one of them kills an ox, he is expected to send his *sahwira* its tail and back, and each time his friend should prepare enough beer for him to use at his *hoka*. This procedure is the same for women.

The formation of a life of friendship or *usahwira* by two women in the Chinamora reserve was described to me by Gwindi, a brother of Chief Chinamora. A married woman with one or two children takes a liking to a woman to whom she is not related. The two women often speak to one another and find their temperaments suited. Each tells her husband she would like the other as her *sahwira*. Eventually one of them takes the initiative. She takes a hen and a basket of ground finger millet to her friend who prepares beer with it. When it is ready the two women and their friends come and drink it at the home of the one who prepared it. Other interested members of the family or friends are invited to the party where the two women pledge loyalty to one another, saying, 'We are friends from now onwards. We shall never separate.' A fowl is killed and its flesh is given to the people to eat by the woman who prepared the beer. Her husband says, 'See, I have just been given this for friend-ship'. Stiff porridge is also provided and when the food has been eaten and the beer consumed everyone returns home.

The ritual is not yet over, for the woman who cooked the hen next brews more beer and invites her friend and her husband to come and drink it. When it is finished both parties return to the village of the first *sahwira* who presented her friend with the millet and fowl. Her husband now leads them to the cattle-kraal and says to the other *sahwira*, 'Here is a beast for you'. This becomes her own property and is taken back to her village by her husband. This takes place at any convenient time after the first beer was brewed. From now onwards the two women are true and permanent friends.

In future whenever one of them obtains something special, such as a good relish, she gives some to her *sahwira*. They often visit one another and if one of them is ill the other gives her a chicken to nourish her.

In the Chinamora reserves the chief duties of a woman to her *sahwira* are to share anything special she has with her, to help her with her tasks, such as brewing beer, and perhaps with weeding her garden. In return she will be sent some of the beer the friend brews. When a woman *sahwira* dies, her friend brings 'cloth' to the hut where she is lying and says, 'Good-bye, I have brought you this *jira* to cover you'. She does not enter the grave to put the body into position as is done by a man; instead her husband does this for her. The surviving *sahwira* does not look for another friend to take the deceased's place, but if her friend leaves daughters behind she considers them her *sahwira*. This is a continuation of the love she bears for their dead mother.

A *nganga* (medicine man) from Manicaland gave me the following account of the formation of a ritual friendship in his district: Two men meet often until one of them brews beer and has a goat and a fowl in readiness and then invites the other *sahwira* and his wife to his village. The fowl and goat are killed and both families enjoy the food and beer. One pot of beer is left for the visitor to take home and there he is joined by his friend and they drink it together. A few weeks later it is the other *sahwira's* turn to invite his friend to his village and to kill a goat and a fowl in his honour. The same ceremony takes place as previously. About two months later the first *sahwira* goes to his friend's village and simply takes one of his goats, but this does not upset its owner as it is part of the ritual cementing their friendship. He can do what he likes with the goat—kill and eat it or merely keep it. A few weeks afterwards the friend retaliates by removing a goat, a cow or an ox from his kraal. A year or so later one of the *sahwira* kills a *mombe* and invites his own and his friend's relations to come and enjoy the meat. Both families meet and celebrate at his village and it sometimes happens that a son of one of the *sahwira* may take a fancy to a daughter of the other and their subsequent marriage will cement the friendship still further.

This type of ritual friendship is known as far afield as

Nigeria where Simmons[1] records it among the Efik of Cala-bar. There it begins during late adolescence or early adult-hood when two young people take an oath of friendship which is strengthened and cemented by each one cutting the other's right wrist.

Mary Tew[2] refers to the blood brotherhood of certain societies. Among the Azande as with the Shona, one of the main obligations of blood brotherhood is the performance of burial rites that are taboo to the kin of the deceased. The pact between the two parties implies that the first who dies is to be buried by the other. Practical jokes are as much part of the relationship as the exchange of gifts. In some tribes a ritual friendship exists between people of the same tribe as well as between members of different tribes.

In Tanganyika every member of a tribe, no matter what age or sex, is by birth the *utani* (friend) of every member of the other tribe. In some societies there is the institution of forfeits whereby if a member of the one tribe meets another of the other tribe associated in this relationship, if he carries some meat in his hand, he forfeits it unless it is covered by a leaf. Similarly if he wears new clothes before they have been washed, these too are forfeited.[2a]

Several valuable papers[3] have been published on what their authors call the 'joking relationship' found among African tribes. This form of association is also a feature of Shona society and is almost peculiar to African society, quite unlike anything seen in European society, although I under-stand that a type of close friendship of this nature between two people exists among Germans. It embodies a state of friendship or understanding between two people, generally men, who are unrelated to one another and thus of different totems. So close are the bonds between them that they are never broken except by death. I think the term 'joking relationship' is perhaps a little unfortunate, certainly as far

[1] Simmons, D. C. *Africa* (1960), *30*, 153.

[2] Tew, M. *Africa* (1951), *21*, 122.

[2a] Moreau, R.E. *Africa* (1944), *14*, 386.

[3] Radcliffe-Brown, A. R. *Africa* (1940), *13*, 195; Tew, M. op cit.; Beattie, J.H. M. *Africa* (1958), *17*, 198; White, C. M. N. *African Studies* (1958), *17*, 28.

as the Shona is concerned, for although joking and teasing are a feature of the association, the emphasis is really on solid friendship rather than on the joking relationship, and this friendship among the Shona is really a ritual friendship (*usahwira*), as described above.

A SPECIAL FORM OF FAMILY INTIMACY OR JOKING RELATIONSHIP

Besides this special friendship there is another form of relationship among the Shona that may be referred to as a joking one and this also implies a certain intimacy between those concerned and exists only among people with a special family relationship. It is a pleasant intimate association and also affords the opportunity of ragging and playing tricks on one another, a more jocose form of the teasing so often seen in European families. This relationship exists among the *varamu*, i.e. between brothers-in-law and sisters-in-law. They are all on the same level, that is of the same generation and if circumstances so arise are permitted to marry. They are thus of different totems. A man is permitted to joke, tease, flirt with or even fondle his wife's sisters although no sexual relationship with them is allowed. He may throw a bucket of water over one of them or may be treated in this manner by one of them. Describing the relationship between in-laws of the same generation, Child[4] was struck by the term '*varamu*' among the Shona. He says, 'these *varamu* may laugh together and all of this term may marry each other. Any male *varamu* is a prospective husband and the converse applies.'

A man can behave in the same way with his brother's wife's sister and daughter as they are included in the same category. Thus this joking relationship takes place only among the members of the immediate family circle who are permitted to marry one another. For instance, if a man's wife dies he may be expected to marry one of the *varamu* and

[4] Child, H. F. 'Etiquette and Relationship Terms', *Native Affairs Department Annual* (1948), 18.

vice versa; if he dies his wife is inherited by one of his brothers. Perhaps the object of this joking relationship is to establish a friendship and intimacy among those who may be required to marry one another at a later date.

On the other hand this sort of intimacy is not permitted between people of a different generation. A man may not joke in this way with his aunts or with his mother-in-law or her sisters. This would be most lacking in respect and regarded as a grave misdemeanour in tribal law. Some workers have found a similar intimacy between grandparents and their grandchildren, but to me this does not appear to be the same type of association. A young child may pull its grandfather's beard, but this is a display of affection and not a joking relationship such as exists among the *varamu*.

White[5] stresses that this joking relationship exists among the Luvale between members of the same generation who call one another *nyali* (brothers-in-law—and sisters-in-law) or cross-cousins (*musonyi*). The *nyali* corresponds to the *muramu* of the Shona. But he includes in the same category the familiarity between grandparents and grandchildren, although the latter are not permitted to tease their grandparents. He also mentions a joking relationship between alternate generations, that is, between a man and the generation above him, such as his father's sisters or his mother's brother's wife, which I have certainly not found among the Shona.

Based on his experience with the Nyoro in Uganda, Beattie,[6] like White, describes an intimate relationship between grandparents and grandchildren in contrast to the father-and-child relationship. The child is permitted to stroke the grandfather's hair, but dare not do this with his father. He may joke with the grandfather, but not with his father. This variety of joking relationship seems to correspond to the asymmetrical type in which only one of the two persons in the relationship teases or makes fun of the other.

In contrast to the demonstration of natural affection

[5] Op. cit.
[6] Op. cit.

A young mother returns to the village carrying firewood. She has also a baby on her back. (see page 22.)

Mother washing her child on a stone in Chikwaka reserve. (see page 33.)

Above: Young boys playing at oxen. (Nyandoro reserve.) (see page 27.)

Left: The *chowe*—long pieces of firewood stacked by the tree—a typical sight in Mashonaland. (see page 26.)

between father and son or grandfather and grandson there is at times a complete avoidance of familiarity between certain other relations. Radcliffe-Brown[7] draws attention to the extreme respect shown between a son-in-law and his wife's parents. There may be complete avoidance of any social contact between a man and his mother-in-law. For instance, among the Luo in Kenya there is a very extensive avoidance which is considered an essential part of the respectful attitude required towards his wife's family (Evans-Pritchard).[8] If a man sees his parents-in-law in his path he makes a detour to avoid them and if he has to speak to them he turns his back on them, especially when addressing his mother-in-law, who also turns her back on him. This avoidance becomes less as the years pass and as more children are born relations between a man and his parents-in-law grow less formal. Evans-Pritchard[9] refers to a ceremony which may be held after the birth of the first child to enable its father to enter his mother-in-law's hut and partake of a meal with her. A goat is brought into the hut. This is reminiscent of the ceremony of *masungiro* which is practised by the Shona, whereby a goat is killed and its flesh eaten by the two couples. This is the first meal eaten together with the bride's parents after the young couple's marriage and has to conform with a special ritual.

Much the same attitude of respect is recorded by Beattie,[10] who defines the relationship among the Nyoro between a man and his wife's family group. This relationship between a man (and his brothers) and his wife's parents is called *buko* and this word implies constraint. It is one of politeness, with formality and restraint on both sides. It must not be forgotten that the man is a generation below that of his father-in-law and his parents-in-law address him accordingly as their child. Margaret Read[11] describes the form of behaviour expected of a bride or young married woman towards

[7] Op. cit.
[8] Evans-Pritchard, E. E. *Africa* (1950), 20, 132.
[9] Ibid.
[10] Ibid.
[11] Read, M. *Africa* (1938), 11, 1.

5

her mother-in-law, to whom she is taught to be extremely submissive.

In Shona society this utmost respect is also displayed by the son-in-law towards his *tezvara* and *vambuya* (father-in-law and mother-in-law) and to their children as well. Even if he is older than one of the *tezvara's* sons, when he meets him, he must always address him first. Before the son-in-law and his wife can carry out the *masungiro* ceremony, which takes place a few months after their first pregnancy, they must avoid talking to, or even seeing, her parents until this ritual begins.[12]

As with other tribes, among the Shona a child is not allowed to play with his mother or father, but is permitted to display his affection towards his grandparents. He must avoid physical contact with his parents, such as showing his face, rubbing himself affectionately against his mother or father, or taking any liberties with either parent. This avoidance rule forbids a son to wash his father's corpse or receive his body into the grave. If there is no *sahwira*, the *vakuwashu* perform these duties.

White[13] also refers to a wider form of friendship, a joking relationship existing between members of different but specific tribes, although not all of them follow this custom. The Shona for instance do not practise this form of friendship. In Malawi members of the Bemba tribe tease and joke with those of the Ngoni, and the Lozi and Ilsa peoples have the same relationship with one another, yet the Luvale have no such connexion with any outside group.

Mary Tew[14] describes this form of intertribal joking relationship between tribal groups in Tanganyika (Tanzania) and Portuguese East Africa. According to her this custom exists between the Zambezi in the south and Lake Tanganyika in the north and from the east coast to the Luangwa River.

I have stressed in some detail the various forms of friendship existing among the Shona. Each type has a different purpose in the society, each in its own way designed to

[12] Gelfand, M. *Shona Ritual* (1959), and *Shona Religion* (1962); Juta, Cape Town.
[13] Op. cit.   [14] Op. cit.

ensure a state of equilibrium or peaceful relationships within the family segment or clan.

PLAYING HARD TO GET

Several of the behaviour patterns of the Shona almost remind one of the joking relationship. The average European girl, when first told by a young man of his love would not reject her suitor with the words, 'Get out of here, you horrible man! If not I shall tell my father to order you out.' She would refuse him more politely or try to avoid the issue if she were not interested in his advances and accept them readily if she were. But the traditional African girl who accepts the first approaches of a potential husband is unlikely to win him. He would consider her cheap and change his mind. The proper procedure is to pretend to lose her temper and order him to leave. No matter how keen she is she informs him she does not love him. She knows that if he really loves her he will return. She rejects him a second or even a third time until, after several approaches have been made, perhaps some months later, she accepts his hand in marriage, provided she is satisfied that he is a good man. But the matter does not rest at that. After she has promised to marry him and has given him her pledge (nhumbi), when his father has consented to the marriage, an intermediary (munyai) is sent to her parents for their approval. And this is not given readily. When the munyai arrives in the village and sends a message to the father informing him of the purpose of his visit, instead of welcoming him, the father and his sons may set upon him and push him about. This is done to show the prospective son-in-law that the girl's father is not anxious to marry off his daughter. The munyai returns to the young man's village and reports on his reception. But, as the young man is in earnest, the intermediary is sent back at a later date to carry on the negotiations. Again we see that the African is not to be rushed into any hasty decisions. He is afraid of lowering his daughter's value by accepting the first offer and prefers to make sure that the person who seeks his daughter's hand is really in earnest.

6 *Manners*

As can be appreciated with such a closely knit society a fixed code of manners is essential to avoid friction. Anyone who knows the African, or has visited his village, is impressed with the meticulous attention given to the correct performance of procedures normally attributed to 'custom', in which manners constitute a significant part. Wilson[1] considers that there are four aspects to be dealt with under the term. Custom and manners are an important conception. The others are morality, largely developed by religion, common policy, sanctioned by rewards and punishments in the group, and lastly, the law sanctioned by inquiry followed by compulsion or punishment. In the traditional society of the Shona exemplary manners take a high place. If there is justification for the saying 'Manners maketh man', it certainly applies to this society. Many workers have observed the emphasis placed on correct behaviour. For instance Munday[2] comments on the great care taken to teach the African child correct behaviour. Each girl and boy receives a thorough training in family relationships, the love of agriculture and of medicine. This training does not take place at school, but in the home and village where the child learns by example. Margaret Read's[3] researches into the moral code of the Ngoni in Nyasaland is of particular interest, as in this particular society the code of behaviour is similar to that found among the Shona, particularly with regard to their sexual practices. Child[4] provides us with a clear description

[1] Wilson, G. *Africa* (1936), 9, 75.
[2] Munday, J. T. *Native Affairs Department Annual* (1942).
[3] Read, M. *Africa* (1938), 11, 1.
[4] Child, H. F. *Native Affairs Department Annual* (1948), 18.

of the etiquette and relationship terms among the Ama-
ndebele in Matabeleland, also very similar to those of their
neighbours the Shona. He points out how naturally polite
the African is, especially to his elders. Respect for certain
relatives is also clearly expected. For instance it is considered
very bad form for an *unmarried* woman to eat in the presence of her future mother-in-law or father-in-law, or to
use the names other than totem names of those related by
marriage.

In a society with a sense of discipline and respect for others
we can anticipate that the people have good manners. For
instance I should like to mention the charming way in which
a visitor is bade farewell. When the time comes for him to
take leave, the villagers do not say good-bye at the entrance
to the village, but his host, and often a small group of people,
accompany him for about half a mile or so along his route in
order to ensure that he is travelling in the right direction.
If this were not done it would be considered a slight to the
visitor. It is important to show attachment to, and interest
in, a friend to the very last possible moment. It shows the
warmth of feeling and pleasure in having had this person
to stay in the village.

One of the most common acts in everyday life is the
receiving of an article, and it is most important to do so
correctly. No matter whether the recipient is old or young,
if the gift is large or insignificant, the person receiving it
must first clap both hands quietly and briskly once or twice
and then extend both palms placed alongside each other
with the fingers slightly crossed so that the two hands
together assume the rough shape of a spoon ready to receive
the article. The only exception to this is a husband receiving
his food at the *dare* from his wife. In this case there is no
need to clap hands as his family has already paid for this
attention in bridewealth.

Whenever a person wishes to greet someone or make his
presence known he claps both hands a few times. Men clap
hands slightly obliquely palm to palm so that the flat of one
hand meets that of the other. The male clap is known as

kubonda. The female clap is different as the palms meet one another at right angles and slightly concave. This is known as *kubobodza*. The number of claps varies, but for ordinary occasions there may be three or four short fairly brisk ones with two seconds between each. If an important person, like a chief, is to be received, the procedure is different. All the men sit on the ground, clap twice and are then silent for ten seconds, after which there is a very quick succession of claps, lasting for about a minute.

It is more correct to greet a person sitting down. The legs can be in any position, but when a son-in-law greets his father-in-law they must be tucked under him. When an African addresses another or delivers a message to him it is preferable for both parties to be sitting on the ground. Business is never discussed standing, but always sitting.

Hands are not shaken ordinarily, but only when the occasion lends itself and then only if an acquaintanceship has already been established. Women shake hands in the same way as men. The correct method of shaking hands (*kumbundirana*) is a forceful downward movement after the hands have been gripped. The so-called 'Chaminuka handshake' is a recent innovation. Each person grips hands in the ordinary way, then releases the grip and the person who initiated the procedure grips his friend's thumb and then he does the same. This is repeated three times. The nephew (*muzukuru*) may shake hands with his aunt (*vatete*) and her husband, but if he has not seen his grandmother for some time he greets her by throwing his arms round her chest (*kugumbatirana*) and she responds in similar fashion.

When a granddaughter (*muzukuru*) greets her grandfather (*sekuru*) she kneels, shakes hands and then claps her hands. A grandson does not kneel when he greets his grandfather. First he embraces him (*kugumbatirana*) then removes any weapons or implements he may be wearing, claps his hands, half bends his knees and shakes the grandfather by the hands and leads him into the main hut.

If two unmarried women greet one another they shake hands, semi-incline their knees and then clap hands. One says 'Makadii Shumba' and the other replies 'Tiripo Tsoko', thus giving the mitupo of their fathers. When two male friends greet each other they shake hands and each says 'Mhoro shamwari', then they release their hands and clap them. They then both sit down, clap hands together again, one saying, 'Makadii Nyamuziva' and the other replying 'Tiripo Mrewa' (We are well). When two women friends meet they behave in the same way as the men. If one of them is married to a man whose mitupo is Shumba and his chidao is Nyamuziva, the greeting is 'Makadii Nyamuziva' (thus mentioning the chidao of the husband). A man greeting another says 'Kwaziwai chirombohwe' or 'Kwaziwai mhanduwe' and the other answers 'Evoyi chirombohwe'. Then the first says 'Makadini kumusha kwenyu?' (How are you at home?) and the second replies, 'Kutsvene hako' (All is well), 'Kwakanaka zvako', Kwakanaka zvavo' or 'Kamwana kanhingi kari kurwara' (but the child of so and so is sick).

The whole greeting process is usually carried out in a slow and deliberate manner. Let us imagine some men are sitting at the dare (the place in the village where they congregate) and another arrives. As the newcomer approaches the circle of men, he stops and sits down just outside it. As he sits he claps his hands gently two or three times and then remains sitting absolutely quietly. The most senior man at the meeting-place stops talking, but the rest continue with their business or chat undisturbed by the arrival. The visitor waits for a break in the conversation, when he claps his hands again three or four times fairly slowly but not too loudly. The senior man replies by clapping. This denotes that he is welcome to stay and to tell them the reasons for his arrival.

A woman's greeting is different from that of a man. For instance if she passes a man on the path or near the place where he is sitting or if she passes a more senior woman, she claps hands in the female manner, at the same time stopping in her course and curtsying by quickly bending both knees and inclining them to one side. A man does not curtsy except when he greets a very senior woman, such as

his grandmother. A woman often curtsys when handing
something to a man. She may kneel when approaching or
handing over something to a senior man such as her husband or an important person in the tribe. For instance a
woman or her daughter approaching the husband or father,
who is seated on the ground, either to hand him an article or
to discuss a matter, first kneels, claps her hands and then
begins to talk or, after kneeling with her head well bent,
gives him with both hands his food or whatever she has
brought him. It is still a common practice in the Shona
village today for a wife and daughter to kneel to the husband
and father.

Whenever a visitor comes to a village, especially if he is a
person of some standing in his society, the women show their
pleasure in his arrival by going out to meet him on the
entrance path or by waiting for him to pass them at the
entrance to the village, shrilling while the men gathered
there clap their hands. This spontaneous action demonstrates
the warmth of their welcome.

For a special occasion when men wish to show their
appreciation to an honoured person, or to a spirit, the special
handclap used is known as *gusvi*. The hands are more widely
separated—about 15 inches apart and then brought together
in a louder clap than the ordinary one already described. On
such occasions the women do not clap, but shrill instead.

No European visitor can fail to be touched when, in the
course of his visit to a village or just before his departure,
the headman asks his wife or one of the children to catch a
fowl and hand it to the guest. This gift may come at any
moment, usually unexpectedly and spontaneously. Sometimes it is not a fowl, but some eggs or other produce, such
as a pumpkin. This is a token of the host's appreciation of the
visit and indicates that not only is the visitor held in high
regard, but also with affection. This is a typically African
expression of hospitality.

Whenever a visitor calls at a village he should be given
something to drink, such as beer or, nowadays, tea. It would
be the height of discourtesy for the villagers to omit this

and equally as rude for the guest to refuse to take something offered to him. It is also customary for a visitor to bring a token or small gift for the family, and to hand it over to the father or mother.

THE TRAINING OF A BOY

The mother, more than any other person, teaches her little boy manners. She concentrates on the manners expected of a man, but does not forget that he must be taught how to conduct himself generally in society. As soon as he can walk she shows him how to greet his father by clapping his hands lengthwise and saying: '*kwaziwai baba*'. She holds his hands and shows him how to do this. When he can greet his father properly she teaches him how to greet visitors, while an older child pretends to be the visitor. She explains that the boy must not kneel like a girl, but must sit down in front of the visitor inclining his knees and hips so that the knees touch each other. Although he does not kneel when greeting a senior man, a boy may bend his knees slightly to one side while clapping hands to greet his grandfather or grandmother.

From about the age of 8 his mother sends him on messages to other huts. She tells him to clap hands at the entrance, but not to go inside until the woman invites him into the hut. Then he must enter, sit down, wait a minute and then clap his hands. If they are close neighbours the woman does not greet him, but merely asks why he has been sent to her. He then tells her the reason. He may have come to borrow a little salt for his mother, or some fire. The woman or her husband puts some burning embers (*zimbe*) into a piece of broken clay pot and hands it to him to take home. He must clap his hands first and then hold them both out to accept it.

From about 15 to 20 years of age the boy is expected to greet any elder of a village, who happens to be walking along a path, by stepping aside and half inclining his knees, clapping his hands and saying '*Tipfuure zvedu chirombowe*'

(May we pass). He remains in this position until the senior man has passed. The procedure is the same for a senior woman, but not for his father-in-law or mother-in-law. He must sit down cross-legged and clap his hands to greet his parents-in-law because of the great respect due to them. Whenever a boy inquires after the health or welfare of a senior man or woman from this person, he must clap his hands before introducing the subject.

When two people greet one another, the younger person must always ask first how the older one is. Failure to do this denotes bad upbringing. The only exception to this is that the son-in-law must always speak first when greeting any member of his father-in-law's family, no matter how old or young this person is. But this respect is mutual. For instance if the son-in-law meets his wife's grandmother, she kneels, he sits down, and both clap hands for a few moments before they talk to each other. This practice is strictly adhered to no matter when or where they meet.

There is also a very strict code of manners for the *dare*. No boy eating at the *dare* with his father and other elders would presume to begin before the men have started. Nor must he finish his food and start walking away before his seniors. Even if he has had sufficient, he must still chew a morsel of food very slowly while they are still eating, for if he were to rise and leave, or even stop eating, this would be considered the height of disrespect to his seniors. When everyone has finished, one of the young boys collects the plates and carries them to his mother to wash.

After passing beyond the age of being regarded as small children, boys have very little contact with their sisters or other girls. Margaret Read[5] described this among the Ngoni. She mentioned that when a boy began to cut his second teeth he moved around exclusively with other boys of the youngest group. 'All the tests of hardness and endurance, all the schooling in obedience and discipline of a communal living were enforced by the older boys and all aimed at making a warrior.'

[5] Op. cit.

Yet although the moral code and ethical conduct are given greater stress than in European society there seem to be territories in Africa in which these appear to be lax. For instance, Culwick[6] states that it is common knowledge that in some Bantu tribes sexual intercourse in one form or another begins before puberty for the majority of children. In some places for as long as the people can remember it has been the accepted practice for girls to have full sexual intercourse for several years before their first menstruation. Yet Culwick finds these same people shut the girl away in rigorous confinement the moment she reaches puberty. I can only quote my experience among the Shona which has been completely different from his; among them this is absolutely foreign to their code of behaviour.

THE TRAINING OF A DAUGHTER

The Shona woman, as Sloan said, is very concerned with her home, her husband, his relations and friends. She observed that among the people of the Dande (near Mt. Darwin) there was no such person as a lone woman. The woman showed a tenderness to all young children and derived a whole-hearted pleasure in them. Sloan was impressed with the graceful way in which the woman placed the food before her husband and with the polite way in which he clapped his hands as she did this. After putting down the food she clapped her hands and dipped a curtsy from the knees, holding her head and back straight.

The manners of a Shona woman can only be described as beautiful and in keeping with the personality of a woman. From this it is clear that a girl must receive as careful and strict a training in manners as does a boy.

From an early age she is taught by her mother or grandmother to kneel (*kupfugama*) and clap her hands crosswise at the same time saying, '*Kaziwai shewe*' or '*Evoi chirombowe*'. She is told to practise this with her elder sisters and brothers until she can do it perfectly. Whenever she hands *sadza* or

[6] Culwick, G. M. *Africa* (1939), *12*, 425.

water to her father or grandfather she claps her hands (*kubobodza*). Whenever there are adults in the hut she must clap her hands saying '*Tishore*', a phrase that denotes her willingness to help. When greeting an adult she must bend her knees slightly to the side at an angle of about 20° (*kutyora muzura*) at the same time clapping her hands. When handing food to a man she must kneel first. This is specially important when a woman takes food to the *dare*. She kneels before her husband, hands him the plate of *sadza* and the small pot containing vegetables and relish, but he does not clap in acknowledgement. She rises and returns to the imba.

If a girl of 10 years, or older, meets a senior person (even a stranger) on a path, she moves off, sits down with her knees apart, her legs folded under her and crossed at the ankles and claps her hands saying '*Tipfuurewo*'. The man she is greeting is probably carrying his axe, spear or knobkerrie. He places this on the ground, bends his knees with one leg slightly behind the other and claps his hands saying, '*Evoyi mukweguru*'. The child replies, '*Maokoi shewe*'. The adult inquires: 'How are all the people at home?' and the girl, still clapping her hands, answers: 'They are all well', and then asks 'How are the people at your home—are they all well?' If she meets an elderly woman or even an adult woman or a young man she behaves in the same way, except that she kneels, almost touching the ground, instead of sitting. Every time she meets one of her parents outside the village she should bend her knees slightly, clap hands and say '*Tipfuurewo baba*' (or '*amai*'). Her mother drills her carefully in this routine until she is sure she knows what to do for every occasion.

Every young girl is taught how to receive an article correctly (*kuombera* or *kubobodza*). She first claps her hands three or four times, then extends them both, palms upwards, touching each other, but if the person from whom she is receiving it is someone she respects highly, such as her father, she kneels first. When one of her parents sends her to fetch something, she kneels on both knees as she hands it over with both hands. The parents receive it, clapping hands and

saying 'Maita mwana'ngu' (Thank you, my child). To his
adult daughter the father says 'Maita mukewguru'.

The child is taught how to receive and address visitors and
also how to behave as a visitor herself. Let us imagine she
has been sent on an errand to someone in the same or in a
neighbouring village. When she reaches her destination she
stops in the doorway of the hut and claps hands. The woman
inside claps her hands saying, 'Kaziwa mwana'ngu' (Greetings
to you, my child). If the husband happens to be present he
then greets the visitor, clapping his hands and saying, 'Kaziwa chirombowe', and the child replies 'Kaziwa chirombowe'. If
one of the daughters of the family is present, she rises,
kneels and claps hands, saying, 'Kaziwa chirombowe', and the
little visitor acknowledges her presence by clapping hands
and answering, 'Evoyi mukweguru'. Next the daughter of the
family inquires respectfully after the health of the visitor's
family and she replies accordingly. It is now the turn of the
woman to clap hands and ask how the visitor's relatives are.
If the visitor is an adult and happens to be a highly respected
man, such as a chief or headman, who hopes that one day his
son will marry a daughter of the family, the procedure is a
little different. In this instance, after the daughter has
inquired after his family, instead of her mother asking again,
the visitor poses the next question.

When a child is instructed in the use of the terms chirombowe, shewe, mhanduwe, she is told to use them only if she
does not know the person's totem (mutupo). But if the
mutupo and chidao (praise name) are known, if, for example
the mutupo is Moyo and the chidao muzukuru, the girl is
taught to greet the visitor with 'Kaziwai Moyo', and the
visitor replies, 'Wakadii muzukuru' or 'Nyama muzukuru'.

It should not be imagined that people meeting one another
regularly in a village go round clapping hands and curtsying
all day. There are the special occasions, such as when food is
brought to the dare, a gift is given, or someone wishes to
show his appreciation of another. Otherwise for people
constantly living together no greeting is needed other than
the usual good morning, good evening or good night. If

the father or mother has been away from the village for a day there is a special greeting for him or her on returning. The girl kneels when she first sees them. To the father the child says 'Kaziwai baba' and to the mother 'Kaziwai amai', and they reply in similar fashion. Then the child asks after the people they have been visiting and says, 'Ko, maswera zvakadii?' (How did you spend the day; how are the people at the village you visited?' The parent replies 'Vakasimba zvavo' (Those we visited are well).

Reception of Visitors

A married visitor is given his own room, whereas a young boy or girl sleeps with the unmarried sons or daughters of the village. The head of the family sends one of his sons or daughters to prepare a fire in the hut and to take a sleeping-mat (rukukwe) and a blanket for the use of the guest. It is not usual for a visitor (mweni or muenzi) to bring his own mat and blanket. All a male visitor carries is his spear or axe, whereas a woman brings with her a basket filled with meal, meat or any other food she thinks her friends may enjoy. The head of the village should kill a fowl or a goat for relish for the guest. This applies also when a father-in-law or son-in-law comes to the village, but for a son-in-law, only a fowl is provided, and never a sheep or goat. The living animal is presented to the guest by the head of the family, who tells him it is for relish. Then the visitor asks him to kill it for him (or her). When it is cooked by the woman of the house she gives the pot of cereal to the guest to serve with the relish. A male cannot do this so he hands it to his wife to do for him. If he has come without his wife, one of the women in the village is delegated to carry out this service for him. Everyone partakes of the meal with the visitor in the main hut, but the men and women sit in separate groups. After having eaten, the guest repairs to his own hut to sleep, but he has all his meals in the main hut, unless he stays for longer than three days, after which he joins the other men at the dare. A woman of course eats in the main hut for the duration of her stay, sharing the same plate as the woman of the house.

When a man arrives on a visit to a village he goes straight to the *dare* and sits down. In the meantime the head of the family sends one of his children to inform the wife of the guest's arrival. At the same time the child relieves the visitor of any article he is carrying and takes it to the main hut for him. The visitor sits at the *dare* for a while talking to the men and then goes to the main hut where his hostess is waiting to receive him. Sometimes she comes out to the meeting-place to greet him, kneeling in front of him and clapping hands. After greeting him she returns immediately to the main hut where he soon follows her. If he is a relation of her husband, such as a brother or nephew, the woman must clap her hands (*kubobodza*) first and ask how he is, but if he is not related he claps hands first. A woman visitor on the other hand does not go to the *dare* when she arrives, but straight to the main hut. Her hostess then sends a daughter or son to inform her husband that a visitor has arrived, and he comes to the hut to greet her and ask after the people at her village. After talking to the visitor for a little while he returns to the *dare*.

Greeting (*kuuchira*) is carried out according to the status of the visitor, especially if he is a relation. If the visitor has a special reason for having come to the village he mentions its nature when he first comes to the *dare*, but he must discuss it only in the main hut.

At the end of his stay the visitor takes leave of his friends and tells them that he is returning to his own village. This procedure is called *kunoneka*. When he leaves the village, as mentioned earlier, a member of the village accompanies him for a short distance along his path. This is done whether he is married or unmarried. When a woman visitor leaves, she is given a basket with some food in it, such as groundnuts or dried meal to take with her. She must bring this back to her own village, because if she returns with an empty basket it means that the people with whom she stayed were not pleased with her visit. A male guest returns only with his own weapon that he took with him.

7   *Procedure*

Included in the term of Procedure are a few important methods adopted when the Shona wish to draw a particular matter to the notice of another person. Thus we encounter what I have termed the 'indirect approach' or the 'buffer system'. Then there is the matter of 'reciprocation' and 'compensation', which come into play as the result of certain acts. Included in this chapter would be the quality of *preciseness* which is displayed by the Shona. When faced with an urgent matter which should be resolved, the individual is incapable of containing himself and thinking clearly and resorts to enforcing a confession from the accused, the actual process frequently becoming a painful procedure. In such a closely knit world, procedure and its correct observance are essential to the avoidance of friction both within and without the family.

The Shona is almost obsessed by correct procedure or protocol and so at all functions the duties of everyone taking part are clearly outlined. Each person knows what *mukuwasha* has to do; what is required of *muzukuru* or niece; who says the prayer; who speaks first and who has to report progress to the father of the family. In European society formal procedure is carefully planned for civil or official functions, but not so meticulously where family matters are concerned. Often, as a result, some members of the family become offended because of the position accorded them at table. In Shona society this cannot happen as everyone knows exactly the order of precedence for each person and so is able to meet the others on all occasions without anyone being hurt. Judging by the universality of procedure throughout Mashonaland, the correct procedure has been laid down

A woman has come to collect water at the well. (Chikwaka reserve.) (see page 29.)

One of the duties of the female is to collect thatch. (Chikwaka reserve, central Mashonaland.) (see page 28.)

A mother carrying her baby on her back in the traditional way. (see page 30.)

A woman carrying her pot which she has just filled with water at the well. (see page 28.)

by tradition and this strict sense of procedure and discipline in Shona life can be compared to that existing in our royal or diplomatic circles. It is ingrained in this society.

Here is an example of an ordinary beer gathering in the Chinamora reserve. The owner of the village appoints a man to share out the pots of beer according to the number of men from the district and the number belonging to the family of the medium of the tribal spirit. The women too are given their share after the visitors have received theirs, and other pots are divided among the men according to their age. The pots are all shared out until they are finished, but the last pot, called the *maharadzo* or *chionano*, is kept for just before everyone leaves for home. The man appointed to organize the distribution of beer is called the *mukokeri* (or inviter) and can be anyone in the village, but is usually a son-in-law. He tells the people collected at the *dare* when the beer is ready after the wife of the man who is providing it has taken him into the hut where it is kept. She gives him a pot which he is permitted to take to his own home if he wishes.

Let us imagine that the beer is being given in return for help with weeding the gardens. After receiving his pot of beer the *mukokeri* tells the people gathered at the *dare* that they must all go to the fields. There they sit while he addresses them as follows: 'This is your *hari*' (pot), and then explains why it is being given. This *hari* is called *chikumura mabachi* which means the beer being given before the helpers take off their coats to start weeding or ploughing. After drinking this pot of beer they work until afternoon when the *mukokeri* provides more beer called *chionano*. He must drink the first cup of beer (*mukombe*) from the pot. This is often not quite clear and may even contain cockroaches or flies floating on its surface. It is thus called the *mapete omukuwasha* (cockroaches of the son-in-law). He gives the next drink to the man he has chosen to help him distribute the beer. After these preliminaries the first helping usually goes to the headman (*sabuku*), the next to the person next in order of precedence to him, known as *gota redu*. The next helpings go to the chief's counsellors and after them to the grandfather (*sekuru*) of the family, the father (*baba*) and the eldest son of the father's sister (*muzukuru*). Then it is distributed from man to man in any order.

After the important people have been given their beer he attends to the women, who are sitting to one side, a little distance from the men, and gives them their own pot of beer to drink. He takes this pot to them and says, 'This is the pot of beer for you'. One of the women takes the cup and gives him the first helping to drink (*mapete omukuwasha*). The women then choose one of themselves to serve out the beer and they begin drinking. The first helping is given to the grandmother (*ambuya*), the second to the youngest sister of the father (*vatete*) and the third to the wife of the eldest son (*muroora*). After that there is no special order of seniority.

When it is time for the party to end, the last pots, called *chionano* or *maharadzo*, are produced and the *mukokeri* announces, 'This is your *chionano*'. The people drink them and return to their homes.

Members of every family unit know their duties and their place in society and these are the same in all families. The *muzukuru* (son of the father's sister) is permitted to settle all minor quarrels or differences in the village or in the immediate family circle. It is his right to stop or intervene in any fight and so he is the local peacemaker. Of course if he fails to settle the argument or considers it too serious to handle himself he should refer it to the grandfather or to the headman of the village.

Child[1] stresses the importance of correct procedure when a beast is killed among the Matabele. There were certain definite rules of precedence, as, indeed, I have observed among the Shona.

By this method of 'indirect approach' or what I also refer to as the buffer system, instead of the two parties concerned meeting one another directly, the emotional aspects of any situation are broached by a disinterested person. As a result the individual approached need not commit himself and

[1] Child, H. F. *Native Affairs Department Annual* (1948), 18.

has time to ponder over the matter. This probably avoids friction, for by the time the parties concerned meet one another face to face the initial irritation has passed. This is in keeping with the African's approach to any problem, as he is averse to making a hasty decision. He prefers less haste and likes to think over any matter of moment, taking months or even years in the business of selecting a chief, before coming to the final decision. An excellent example of this is afforded by the procedure adopted when a delegation sets out to obtain advice from the tribal spirit (*mhondoro*) on a matter of concern to the tribe. They cannot expect to speak direct to the medium of the tribal spirit but must first interview his acolyte and explain the purpose of their visit to him. He proceeds to deal with the problem but cannot do so until the tribal spirit enters him and this may take a few nights. So the acolyte informs the delegates that they should remain in the village and wait for the medium to become possessed. No doubt before this occurs the medium thinks over the matter quietly. But even when he becomes possessed, particularly in a very important matter, his spirit may declare that the decision will be given a few months later and that the tribesmen will have to wait for an answer from the spirit world.

The same delay in giving an answer is seen when a patient arrives to consult a *nganga*. The diviner does not see him at once. First the patient or his relations interview the acolyte and tell him the purpose of their visit and then wait while the latter consults with the *nganga*. More often than not they are told the *nganga* will see them the next morning and they are quite happy to wait for his spirit to possess him in his sleep and so provide the answer they are seeking. This of course gives the *nganga* the opportunity to think over the matter.

I remember an occasion two years ago when the medium of the very powerful tribal spirit Chaminuka stayed at my home in Salisbury. His visit created much excitement, for in his society he has a status comparable to that of an arch-bishop. Therefore it was not a great surprise to me when I heard from the Broadcasting Corporation that they would like very much to have an interview with him if he would agree to speak on the air. Their officials came to my house to ask the medium if he would consent. The latter was unable to give his answer immediately and declared he would have to wait until his spirit entered him to tell him what to do. About six months later, on his next visit to Salisbury, he expressed his willingness to speak on the air, as his spirit had now given him permission.

We meet the same procedure when a girl starts to menstruate: she reports to her aunt (*vatete*) instead of to her mother. This is a delicate matter which the mother may find embarrassing to explain to her daughter. If the girl mentions it to her mother she usually suggests that she discuss it more fully with the aunt. In traditional society the girl would be likely to marry a few years later, so this is an excellent opportunity for the aunt to explain sex and married life, stressing the importance of maintaining her virginity until then. The girl is instructed about the sexual act and her submissive role in the affair.

In the same way when the parents are arranging their son's marriage with the girl's parents the families avoid seeing one another on the first occasion when there is always the possibility of the breaking down of negotiations. The go-between (*munyai*) has the delicate task of bringing the two groups together. By the time he has discharged his duties a feeling of friendship has been established between the families. The difficult stage of bargaining is over and the payments for the bride have been settled, so when the families meet the young man's father is satisfied that his son is marrying into a suitable family and the girl's father has obtained a satisfactory *roora* for his daughter. The intermediary has served his purpose of being a buffer between them and has taken the shocks and discomforts of the negotiations which, as a disinterested party, involve him in no emotional strain. Having brought the couple together successfully he can withdraw from the scene.

Whenever an individual wishes to see an important or

greatly respected person, such as the chief or the medium of a tribal spirit, the procedure is not to approach him directly but first to interview a lesser official and to explain the purpose of the visit and ask to see him. In this way the person concerned has time to think the matter over before meeting the visitor or delegation and committing himself.

In a less important sphere, we notice the same buffer system at work when a visitor comes to the village so that he becomes acquainted with this new group of people gradually. When a man first arrives he does not have his first meal at the men's eating-place (*dare*) but eats in the main hut with his host's wife for a few days and becomes acquainted with her husband and other members of the family gradually, so that by the time he joins them at the eating-place his shyness has been overcome and he is ready to talk to them and eat with them without any inhibitions.

I also like to think that the *sahwira* or the ritual friend answers the need for comfort and advice from a disinterested but trusted person in times of doubt and tribulation. On such occasions it is easier for a man to discuss his troubles with someone outside his kinship group. In this way the *sahwira* becomes a buffer between his friend and the other parties more directly involved, thus affording him the opportunity to release his pent-up emotions. In European society there is no ritual friend, so often a man has no one outside his family whom he can trust for advice, encouragement and support.

I was recently asked by a class of Shona students whether the African conception of God is the same as that of the Christian. I thought not, because while the Shona believe in God, they do not pray to Him and look upon Him as the Creator rather than as One who is concerned with the problems of each individual on this earth. I pointed out that the usual approach was to the *vadzimu* (ancestral or guardian spirits) and to the tribal protecting spirits (*mhondoro*). A Catholic Father, who happened to be present at the same time, disagreed with me, pointing out that he believed the African thought in terms of God in much the same way as

Europeans, but, according to African custom, considered they could not go direct to Him as He was so important, but should approach Him indirectly. It would be wrong to say that a Shona never speaks to his chief, because he never addresses him directly, so it is wrong to say that the Shona never speaks to God, just because he never addresses Him directly but only through the *mudzimu* or *mhondoro*. He added that it is not true that the Shona never speaks directly to God; in a moment of high emotion, for example at the burial of a near relation, the bereaved speaks scoldingly to God: '*Mwariwe ndaite sei?*' he cries. (O God, what did I do to deserve this?)

This is an interesting point of view, although it does not explain the fact that the Shona do not address God in prayer. Further, they believe that sickness and even death may be caused by the family spirits when they are angry about some personal matter and, as a result, any sacrifice or offering is made directly to these spirits, without any reference to God.

RECIPROCATION

In the early days before European occupation, when a white man arrived at a chief's village, he was usually unable to understand the African's request for a gift from him. Sometimes he was annoyed at his demands and considered he was greedy and taking advantage of him. This difference in outlook frequently led to bitter feelings or even arguments, for the visitor could not understand why he was obliged to give the chief something before he left.

This custom is still prevalent throughout African society today, and it is because the African believes that some sort of tangible appreciation should be made whenever a service is rendered. It does not matter how little the person has exerted himself, but even if he has spent time in talking he feels he has made an effort and should be given something in return. In his eyes, even a glance means expenditure of energy and requires something in return. In European society a payment or present is often, although not always, in proportion to the effort made. The more a person does the greater the reward; at least the reward depends on how much the receiver of a service values it. Among Africans of the traditional type, I have been struck by the many customs which display the principle that no matter what a person does for another, some form of appreciation must be shown. For instance, no person would dream of attending a beer ceremony without giving a small token of appreciation. It need not be much, as long as something is given to the person responsible for the ceremony. This applies especially to religious ceremonies. The present may take the form of a basket of millet (*rukweza*), a bangle (*ndarira*) or a small coin, but something must be produced.

We see this principle again at work in marriage ceremonies when the future father-in-law (*tezvara*) arrives at the young man's village to inspect the cattle to be given to him as part of the marriage contract. Certain essential ritual payments have to be made to him. For instance he is paid something for climbing the fence of the cattle-pen to inspect the cattle. Also, he receives a small sum of money for looking at them. This entails a mere glance, but he must be given a small return for his effort. There is, as well, a little payment to him for driving the cattle home to his village. For every little act, a small appreciation is expected.

As mentioned before, every person who attends a religious ceremony must make a sacrifice which usually takes the form of a gift. It is usually small, as it is really a token of the person's sincerity. For example, when attending a rain ceremony at the *muhacha* tree the visitor is careful to give the acolyte a little gift of some snuff or even a small coin. Indeed little presents are given at any ceremonial occasion whether an important or unimportant one. Even at a *shave* dance each person present hands over a token to the medium in whose honour the dance is being held. When a man decides to settle in a new district he is expected to call on the acolyte of the medium of that area to introduce himself and in so doing hands him a little present for the medium. When a person plants maize or pumpkins for the first time on any part of his land, the first fruits must be cooked in a new pot (*tsaiya*) and given to the tribal spirit. The pot is left under the tree for it.

The interesting ritual of *masungiro* among the Shona affords another example of this principle of reciprocation. This ceremony is usually performed up to three months after marriage, provided the bride was a virgin. This ritual is a thanksgiving by the son-in-law to her parents for her purity. On the day selected by the young couple they take a she-goat, its kid and a he-goat to the woman's parents. These animals are provided by the young man's father. During the rather complicated ceremony that takes place the he-goat is killed and special medicine added to the portion of meat which is eaten only by the young wife. Her parents partake only of the meat to which medicine is not added. The she-goat and kid are given to the young woman's mother to recompense her for the medicines she gave her daughter as she grew up and for the trouble she took with her upbringing (*maputiro*), particularly for the blankets soiled by the girl when she was an infant. On the other hand, I might mention, if the bride happened not to be a virgin she would be returned to her father and remain at his village until he and the young husband had arranged what compensation the father should pay the young man. So the principle of reciprocation works in this instance too.

The marriage ceremony (*kuroora*) among the Makorekore displays other instances of this principle. For instance there is the procedure of *binza* carried out after the girl's father has been paid his *roora*. This entails the gathering of the young man's family at the girl's village to assist in the field, weed the gardens, uproot trees and thatch any of his huts that need repairing. This is a nominal recompense to her parents for what it must have cost them to bring her up and to make good the loss they will sustain when she leaves them.

When the son-in-law arrives at his father-in-law's village, as with any other visitor, it is customary to present him with a fowl. It is then cooked by his mother-in-law who gives the pot of cooked meat to the *vatete* (youngest sister of the father of the young wife). The stiff porridge is sent to her too. When it is nearly ready the aunt sends for her niece's husband and hands him the pot of meat saying, 'This is your meat, that your father-in-law killed and cooked for you'. She asks him to divide the meat, which, with the porridge, he shares with his wife's sisters (*varamu*). When they have eaten, the sisters collect the plates and then hand water to the young husband to wash his hands. He then presents a gift of a bangle (*ndarira*) to the aunt, placing it in her relish pot (*mbiya*). This gift denotes his appreciation of having received his wife from his father-in-law. On the other hand when the *tezvara* (father-in-law) visits the village of his *mukuwasha* (son-in-law) he is not expected to provide a gift in return because he has already given the family his daughter. It may seem a bit difficult to understand why a visitor to the village, when given a fowl, makes no such gift after eating it, but I think this is because he has already given the villagers the pleasure of his company and the fowl is an acknowledgement of this.

A similar situation arises when the *muroora* (new wife) first comes to her husband's village. First she goes to the hut of her husband's *vatete* (aunt) where everyone gathers to greet her. Her husband's parents provide a fowl in her honour. This is handed to her husband's aunt (*vatete*) who gives it to the aunt of the new wife (*muroora*), who has accompanied her to the village. The latter hands it back to the husband's aunt to be killed. The husband's mother cooks the fowl and sends one of her daughters with the pot of the cooked meat to the aunt (*vatete*) of the village, who once more hands it to the new wife's aunt, who tells her her meat has come. The young wife remains silent, so her aunt repeats the information, but again she does not reply, so her aunt turns to her husband's aunt and explains that she cannot give her meat as she has refused to talk. Thereupon the latter returns to his parents to tell them that the young wife wants a bangle (*ndarira*) in return for sharing the meat. They hand over a bangle to the aunt who takes it back to the hut where the *muroora* is still sitting and presents it to her aunt. The young wife's aunt now dishes out the meat for her taking care to leave some for the husband's family. They wash their hands, ready to eat, but the young wife refuses to have anything until her husband is called. He arrives, but she still does not eat until he offers her a bangle. Once this ceremony is over, everyone may eat and enjoy the meal. This procedure of offering meat to the young wife who refuses to eat it until she receives the bangles from her parents-in-law and her husband is called *kushonongora muroora*. The young woman has to be shy and coy, sitting with a cloth over her head and only uncovering when she has received the bangles.

At the risk of repetition the details of the marriage procedures as taking place in the Chikwaka reserve today illustrate well the principle of reciprocation. Throughout the account one can detect that a compensation or payment is to be made for certain services rendered.

KUROORA (MARRIAGE)

When a young girl and boy are attracted to one another and have declared their love, she gives him a personal gift called *nhumbi* as a token of her consent to marry him. It may be beads, a bangle or a handkerchief, usually something that she has worn or kept on her person. This may be compared to the engagement ring of Western society, except that it is kept hidden away from the public eye.

The young man takes the *nhumbi* to his aunt (his father's sister) who then goes to his father with it and informs him that his son is in love and gives him the name of the girl. This preliminary period may be defined as one of engagement.

Some weeks later the lover returns to his aunt and tells her that he wishes to marry the girl and would like arrangements to be made for the *pfuma* (part of the bridewealth) to be paid. His father now appoints a go-between (*munyai*), a man, or even a woman, that he trusts, to negotiate with the girl's father. The *munyai* is usually married. He goes to the girl's village to see her father or, perhaps, her uncle and greets him with the customary phrase—'*Ndiri kukumbira sadza*' (I am looking for sadza). After these introductory words he aks the father which daughter it is who is to be married. The father gives her name and the aunt is asked to fetch her. When the girl is brought in to the hut the aunt asks her if she knows from whom the go-between comes, and if she knows the young man. A plate is placed on the ground and the *munyai* gives the father some money which he puts in the plate. The aunt is instructed to take what money she wants from it. She takes some and the father looks to see what is left for him. Nowadays the father would be left about £2, but formerly the payment would be in bangles. This payment is called *rutsambo*. After he has paid *rutsambo* the go-between is told to ask the future son-in-law (*mukuwasha*) for his payment of *pfuma*. This request is relayed to the young man's father, who gives the *munyai* another sum of money—about £5. In former times this payment would have been made in hoes, bangles or fowls. The *munyai* returns with the money, which is still considered part of the *rutsambo*. He is next instructed to produce eight beads as well as a cow for the girl's mother (*mombe youmai*). This part of the bridewealth is called *pfuma* and the cattle are driven to the girl's father by the *munyai*. He returns and reports progress. It is now time for the prospective bridegroom to visit his father-in-law (*tezvara*). At his village he spends two to four weeks helping in the fields or with building. He is given a hut, but is not permitted to sit at the *dare*, although he lights its fire every morning. His food is brought to his hut by his future wife and cooked by her mother. At the end of this period he takes his wife away with him without bidding anyone farewell.

Their journey to his village is a good illustration of the principle of giving something in return for services received. At every stage in the journey the bride (*muroora*) has to receive a gift for walking to the bridegroom's village. As they journey towards it she stops at the first junction of two paths (*mhararano*) and refuses to proceed farther until she has been given a sixpence. They continue until they reach a stream, which she will not cross until he has given her a shilling. Just before the entrance to the village she stops again and the husband goes ahead to tell his aunt of their arrival. She in turn informs his father and all the relations and friends gather to welcome the bride. They go to where she is waiting and welcome her by jumping and shouting and all the men clap their hands. The bride sits on the ground, hiding her face with a cloth, while the people dance around her and hand her a shilling to be allowed to see her face. When she has uncovered it another shilling is presented to her so that she will stand up and walk into the village. After this she proceeds about 5 yards and then refuses to go farther until she is given something. This is repeated every few yards until they arrive at the main hut (*imba yababa.*) At its entrance she sits down again until she is handed another sixpence, when she stands up and goes inside. There, after being given another sixpence, she sits on a reed mat (*rukukwe*) and once more hides her face. Her mother-in-law asks her to uncover herself and offers her another payment for this. After this the relations and friends come into the hut to greet her, but she does not shake hands with them until she receives a small gift. The *vamwene* (mother-in-law) now offers her some *sadza* that she has prepared, but the *muroora* does not accept until she is given another sixpence.

After she has eaten the *muroora* goes to her husband's hut, where she spends the night with him. The next morning she refuses to leave the hut until her husband's aunt gives her a present. She lies on the mat pretending to sleep until the aunt gives her a small coin, after which she leaves the hut and goes to her mother-in-law's room. Early the following morning, she rises and goes round all the neighbouring huts taking to each person in turn warm water and oil with which to wash, and each man gives her a sixpence or a shilling in return. An important person, such as a chief, may give her a fowl.

At this stage in the marriage the *munyai* is sent to the
father-in-law or *tezvara* (bride's father) for what is called
mhere. He takes a hoe or some money with him and is careful
to arive in the village when everyone is sleeping. He
approaches the main hut and throws the money or hoe
(formerly beads) through the doorway, shouting, 'I am so
and so (mentioning the son-in-law's name); I am the one
who has taken your daughter'. Then he disappears. When
he returns to the son-in-law's village the latter's father gives
him a belt and £1 for each of the parents-in-law. He takes
these as well as five shillings for *katso*; that is for the effort
that will be required for the *tezvara* to find a hoe and dig
for medicine. He gives these things to the father-in-law who
instructs him to bring back a beast from his son-in-law (*mombe
yechishava*) and also the young couple. The young couple,
accompanied by the husband's aunt and the go-between,
proceed to his wife's parents for the ceremony of *kusungira*,
taking the ox with them.

When they reach the village the son-in-law and his wife
wait outside while the aunt and go-between take the beast
and present it to the father-in-law, who tells the aunt to
bring the young couple to him. They enter the village and
go into the father-in-law's house. The ceremony of *kusungira*
may take place any time up to about six months after the
marriage.

The following morning the son-in-law kills and skins the
ox and then he, his wife and the aunt sit in one hut while
the meat is cooked in another. The go-between and his party
eat together, and the father-in-law and his wife are given
their share in their own hut and medicine is added to the
meat they eat. The go-between is then given the front leg
of the ox (*bandauko*) for his trouble. He takes leave of the
father-in-law and returns to his village, but the son-in-law,
his wife and his aunt spend a few more days in the village
before going home.

This marriage ceremony as held in the Chikwaka reserve
is basically the same as it was formerly.

After the ceremony of *masungiro* the young wife remains

in her husband's village until she is pregnant, when she returns to her parents for the birth of her first child. She is accompanied by the go-between and her husband's aunt, who hands her father two shillings and asks him to look after his daughter. She remains there until she has had her baby. Immediately after the birth a message is sent to her husband's village to say, 'Your wife has delivered' (*wafurwa nemhepo*). When this news arrives the husband's aunt collects a basket of meal and a pig or goat is killed, and she and the father take these to the father-in-law's village for the sustenance of the mother and infant. When they reach the new village they are not allowed to see the child until they give some money to the maternal grandmother. This is given and the young husband tells his mother-in-law that they have brought food for the new-born. The young mother remains in her father's village for about two weeks after the birth of her child, and then returns to her husband with the infant.

COMPENSATION

Reciprocation is different from compensation. Compensation has to be paid for whatever an African suffers, no matter how slight. 'An eye for an eye, a tooth for a tooth' certainly applies in traditional Shona society. Naturally the greater the loss the greater the payment. For a life the payment may be several oxen, or even a daughter to be married to one of the men of the injured family. But once this payment has been made the two families are completely reconciled. I have already mentioned that some material appreciation is expected for every service or kindness received. The same applies to a loss. The giving of an article is a sign of friendship and goodwill.

For making a mistake, compensation is required. If a *nganga* declares a man or woman a witch, but this person is proved innocent by the ordeal, the doctor must recompense the accused, or the family concerned. The effect on society of this principle is that it makes people extremely careful to avoid giving offence. At all costs a person must not hurt another, and this induces better conduct and smoother relationships between individuals in this society.

An apology is insufficient. There must be a positive effort or sacrifice to show real regret. In European society the expression of regret or sorrow is all that is necessary to restore a damaged relationship, but with the Shona words are not sufficient. For rendering a service, too, words are not enough; payment must be commensurate. A *nganga* expects to be paid for his services. There is a very elaborate system of payment which takes into consideration not only the good he does his patient, but the trouble he takes to search for the herb he uses. The more difficult it is to find the necessary root the greater the payment for this effort. This has nothing to do with the fee for a cure. This is a separate matter and the charge is often very high. If the patient is not cured this fee is waived, as the *nganga* has failed to render a service. He must, however, still be paid for the trouble he took to go to the patient's village and also expects as his right a fowl, or even a goat, to be killed for food for him while he remains with the sick person. This is not given out of politeness but as his due.

Father Hannan has observed that the Shona's outlook on law is different from that of the European as it runs along the same lines as his ideas of compensation. The European expects adequate punishment to be meted to the person who is guilty of an offence. The Shona is less interested in the punishment of the guilty party than in ensuring that the sufferer or offended person or family is fully compensated. To restore the state of equilibrium as speedily as possible, certain payments are laid down by the chief at his *dare* or by the *nganga*. Thus if a person is killed by another the family affected are not satisfied until the person or family responsible has made compensation for the loss. Formerly, once the family of the guilty person handed over a certain number of cattle, or one of their daughters, the case was closed. There was no need to hang or imprison the guilty party. Prisons have never existed in Shona society.

There are many examples of this concept of compensation

to be found in the records of the cases judged by sub-chief Makwarimba in his Court between 1957 and 1960 in the Rusape district. Here are a few examples of those I came across:

Case 22: Nelson had his bicycle, half a bushel of mealies and a jug of milk taken from him by Mumundu, who claimed it as compensation because the former had had sexual relations with his wife. Nelson denied this and said he did not know the latter's wife.

Case 10: Kundeshora demanded his children from Masito, who would not part with them, as he claimed £15 from him for the care he had given the children. Kundishora refused to pay this but was willing to compensate Masito with one ox as he had caused his sister to become pregnant without marrying her.

Case 3: George had slept with Chorumo's daughter without her father's consent and had paid no bridewealth. The girl's father claimed ten fowls, one *mombe yechishava* (ox) and three goats for *masungiro*. The sub-chief ordered him to pay all the demands, except the ten fowls, which he reduced to five.

Case 63: Mhindurwa demanded one *mombe yechishava*, £2 for *masungiro*, £5 in cash from Kamwemba, who had damaged his daughter who was still at school. He also asked for £5 as compensation because she had to leave school.

Case 9494/1/59: Masarurwa committed adultery with Machona's wife while her husband was in prison. Machona demanded five *mombe* from Masarurwa. The *dare* ruled that he was to pay three *mombe* or £15 if he had no cattle. The accused paid £19.

PRECISENESS (KUTSANANGURA)

The Shona likes precise instructions that are clearly understood by all; he dislikes vague orders or commands. This is not only in his relations with the European, but with his own people—man and man, man and woman, woman and woman, adult and child. Whenever anything is to be done

Constructing a shelter for goats in the Nyandoro reserve. (see page 28.)

Preparing stiff porridge in a modern enamel pot. The rest of the cooking and preparation of the food is still traditional. (Photograph taken in Chikwaka reserve, 1964). (see page 34.)

A young boy herding goats in the Nyandoro reserve. (see page 28.)

Leaves of vegetables carried by a young girl to her mother's hut.
(Nyandoro reserve.) (see page 29.)

both sides must clearly understand what is required. Vague-
ness is almost unknown among them. Indeed one of the
criticisms levelled against Europeans by the Shona is that
their orders are too vague and so often matters go wrong
simply because their instructions are not precise and so the
African has to interpret them for himself. Of course this
criticism of the European's lack of preciseness may be due
to language difficulties, and therefore the African's inability
to grasp his exact meaning. This desire to have all details
clear in his mind leads inevitably to delay and long discussion
with much repetition so that all present understand what is
meant.

Related perhaps to his love of preciseness is the great care
taken by the Shona, when introducing a new subject, to
clarify all its details. To us such discussions often appear
long-winded, but the object is to explain to all concerned
what precisely is expected of them. For instance the new
wife (*muroora*), after living and working in her mother-in-
law's hut for as long as three or four years, still has her duties
explained to her very carefully by the aunt (*vatete*) of her
husband when she is first given her own home. Although
these must be very obvious to her after all her training, no
chance is taken and she is still reminded of what is expected
of her.

PATIENCE

A regular visitor to a Shona village cannot help noticing
that nothing is done with great speed and no appointment is
kept promptly. Everything is done in a leisurely manner.
This does not mean that the African is lazy or unwilling to
perform his duties, but that his tempo is slower and more
orderly. Both husband and wife are generally quite active
people, but do not rush about their affairs like people in a
European city. I have often watched African women working
in their huts and gained the impression that they are constantly moving about and fairly busy. There is always something to do, whether preparing the meal or attending to the
needs of the children. The husband also busies himself with

7

various tasks, although he seems to require more rest pauses than his wife. His efforts may not be as substantial as hers, but nevertheless he spends most of his day working on some project.

The African's patience is most evident when he has an appointment. I have often waited at the village meeting-place (*dare*) well beyond the appointed time for the men to congregate. This is very different from the European idea of a fixed time appointment. Europeans work by the clock with an exact time for the beginning and even the ending of an event. I have noticed this attitude in all classes of African society, even among those who have adopted a more European way of life. For instance, I remember the occasion when a number of Africans were invited to an official function in honour of a high dignitary from England. The affair was due to start at 6 p.m. and at that hour a long stream of cars could be seen drawn up outside, and every European was there to the minute. Half an hour later, not an African had arrived, but by 6.40 p.m. they began to appear without the slightest idea that there was anything amiss in arriving so late. I venture to suggest that this lack of hurry on the part of the African is deliberate and designed to protect him from falling into error. Haste brings regret and disappointment.

Such unpunctuality should not be linked with the quality of preciseness, which is referred to as another feature of the Shona. Time is not a matter which is so very important in Shona eyes. Watches, rapid and complicated modes of transport and communication, telegraphy, have only of recent times been made known to them. Further, there is little need to make a hasty decision. The usual appointment is made for late afternoon, daybreak and so on. The exact minutes are not stipulated as is the customary feature of the European. Arriving half to one hour on either side of the clock does not matter.

INTOLERANCE OF TENSION AND CONFESSION

Father Hannan first drew my attention to the Shona's intolerance of a state of tension. Tension within an individual cannot be sustained; sooner or later it bursts out, and so it is fortunate for him that a *nganga* is always available to listen to him and provide the answers to his problems and thus relieve his acute anxiety. The European method of diagnosis or of solving a legal problem is far too slow for the Shona when tension grips him. The length of medical or legal procedure with inevitable delays and debates is foreign to his approach. Thus the *hakata* or the ordeal provides a quick answer and so eases the pressures built up in him. If a man suspects his wife has been unfaithful to him, he must know at once whether to continue sharing the hut with her. To report this matter to the district commissioner and wait for the slow arm of the law to function is useless to him. There is nothing so quick as the boiling-water test. The wife puts her hands into boiling water and if they are scalded she is considered guilty.

If an argument arises between two people and the tension between them becomes too great to bear they find it impossible to wait for an answer. The matter must be settled immediately to relieve acute feelings, or violence may result. The following is an example of this. Chigwaina, aged 40 years, born at Mazoe, was reported to the European authorities[2] by his daughter Vera, aged 16, for assaulting her by placing her head between the prongs of a cleft stick and drawing them together with a bark rope. Her father wanted her to marry a man who had come to their village to ask for her hand and had paid cattle to his prospective father-in-law. The girl refused, but her father insisted that she accept the suitor and ordered her to return to his village with him. After two days she ran away and returned to her father. When she refused to go back to her husband, the father was unable to control his feelings any longer and resorted to this punishment in order to put an end to the argument.

[2] Mazoe D.3/15/4, 14 March 1917. National Archives, Salisbury.

Confession of an individual's sins, malpractices or any antisocial act helps to clear the air and restore the state of equilibrium. In my medical practice I have often come across patients who were told by a *nganga* that their disease was due to their having committed an antisocial act, and in order to be cured they have confessed their wrongdoing. The Shona believes very strongly that unless he confesses the harmful influence will continue to operate against him. It helps his conscience and at the same time pays to admit he has committed an act against society. I well remember an African who became ill with pains and swelling of the abdomen. He lost weight and felt weak. He consulted a *nganga*, who told him he had contracted a disease known as *runyoka* which was caused by committing adultery. The accusation was true and so he confessed his sins, fully expecting to recover from his illness—unfortunately his condition deteriorated and he found his way to the hospital.

I have already mentioned the importance ascribed to confession when a woman has an obstructed labour. This is immediately interpreted as being due to infidelity to her husband and it is firmly believed that unless she confesses the baby will not be delivered. So anxious are those attending her that they may even put her through a form of torture in order to obtain a confession and so save her life and that of the child. A piece of bark or a twig is tied round her head and twisted so that it produces agonizing pain, until her resistance is worn down and she confesses her fault. Everyone is then greatly relieved for they are sure that nature will resume its course and the baby will be born.

Confession is also expected from a woman when her young child becomes ill during its father's absence from the village. As soon as he hears about the illness he rushes home, suspecting that his wife has been unfaithful, but hoping that this is not true. If she has misbehaved, she confesses her misdeeds for she believes this is the only way she can save her child's life.

Confession, too, is a means of relieving tension. If the guilty party confesses and payment is made to the wronged party, the matter is then closed with no ill feeling on either side. The following is an example of this: Magna, an African born in the Lomagundi district, was told that his wife had committed adultery. His own words best describe his state of tension. 'I was told by Chirangwa that my wife was having improper intercourse with Manyembere and if I went to her hut I should find a blanket which Manyembere had given her. I went to her hut and saw the blanket and asked her about it. She said it had been given her by Manyembere. My heart was sore, so I tied her up. She was released on confessing. I tied her to make her confess.'[3]

---

[3] Sinoia D.3/2/2, 1 September 1908. National Archives, Salisbury.

The Fear of Witchcraft

Besides the weights of these family pressures and procedures there is also the fear of witchcraft which tends to
enforce conformity among the Shona. So strong is the belief
in this cult that a number of qualities or attributes are found
well displayed in Shona life. Humility, the readiness to
share, the importance of being of a friendly disposition, all
depend for their effectiveness on an acceptance of witchcraft
belief.

Besides their belief in the tribal spirits (*mhondoro*) and
spirit elders (*vadzimu*) which constitute the spiritual aspect
of their religion, the Shona also consider that there exist
other higher spirits capable of altering the course of nature.
This conception is very real and most prevalent throughout
Mashonaland. Their religion is a proper faith and as clearly
defined as any of the great religions of the world, and I have
already referred to the important effect it has on the attitude
of children and adults towards their grandparents. But the
Shona also have a strong belief in the ability of certain people
on this earth to change things for the good or to the detriment
of others. The person able to bring evil upon others is known
as *muroyi* (witch), and it would not be incorrect to say that
almost all Shona believe that witches have the power to
harm their fellow men. Just as the *mhondoro* and *vadzimu*
represent the positive good in life so do the witches denote
the opposite and take a delight in being bad and harming
others. It is believed that this evil trait enters a person and
possesses him and this evil is within him. It is almost impossible to eradicate it or prevent it from acting through its
host. Thus the witch takes pleasure not only in hurting
strangers but in harming members of his own family.

There are legal records of cases in which the mother or father was accused of killing a child or a relative.

Belief in witchcraft has certain advantages in Shona society, for it tends to produce a well-behaved person. Although other factors contribute towards this good behaviour, there is no doubt that the fear of being classed as a witch prevents many people from antisocial acts.

Most accusations of witchcraft follow the use of threatening language. If some person becomes ill or is overtaken by a catastrophe soon after an argument in which threatening words were used, the chances are that his mishap will be attributed to the person who used these words. This conception is so strong among the Shona that every person is most careful never to give offence or do anything that might lead to an allegation of witchcraft. This is not always possible, as someone is bound to forget himself and make an unfortunate remark in a fit of temper. Similarly fear of witchcraft tends to prevent boasting. The person who is proud of himself and delights in boasting, invites jealousy and, as a result, the allegation that he has used unnatural means to enrich himself beyond normal expectations. A very common fear among the Shona is that a rich or a fortunate man (even an outstanding diviner) is envied by others and thus becomes the target for the attentions of jealous people who try to deprive him of his good fortune and possessions. Obviously, boasting does not pay. The rich man is thus afraid that someone will practise witchcraft against him and so bring sickness and misfortune upon him. Therefore it is better not to be rich or too fortunate in order to avoid provoking the jealousy of others. Witchcraft is thus one of the forces which draws people to the norm. The effect of this endeavour not to display any advantages tends to render the population normal and good and to discourage ambition. To be average or normal is much safer and thus more rewarding in the long run.

Thus the belief in witchcraft ensures good behaviour, modesty and amiability. It produces a uniform type of behaviour and tends to stifle progress and advance in the

Western sense. It also tends to limit friendship with outsiders and to keep it within the confines of the village or
neighbouring villages. People not related, living far away,
are avoided. Someone in distress who comes from afar must
not be befriended lest this stranger is tainted by witchcraft.
This is one of the reasons why charity towards non-kin is not
a feature of African society. It is always possible, in the
minds of these people, that a stranger whose home and
background are unknown may have had a parent who was
a witch. Hence there is a risk in receiving such a person into
the family circle; until his antecedents are known, there is
no fraternization with him. The handshake is not practised
except by people who know each other. Thus when strangers
meet they greet one another by the clapping of hands.
This does not mean that Africans are unkind, but although
they are never rude or disrespectful to someone they do not
know, they are slow in forming a friendship with him and
cautious about taking him to their homes. We see this fear
of witchcraft in African mothers who never leave their
children in the care of strangers. Only relations and people
they know intimately are permitted to touch them. This
also explains her reluctance to leave her baby in hospital.
She wishes to stay there with the child, lest a strange woman,
possessing an evil spirit, touches and brings harm to it.

HUMILITY

The African very seldom boasts. It may be argued that
he has little to boast about, but boasting is largely a relative
matter and is, more often than not, indulged in by the
very people who have fallen a little short of their own
expectations and are driven to show the world that they are
not inferior. In European society we frequently hear people
speak of their own achievements or of the great deeds of
their parents or relatives. Achievement in many different
fields is honoured in diverse ways. Recognition is given in
many different forms to people who deserve it. Perhaps
some societies praise and reward people too easily for their

success and prowess and so some countries strictly limit their distribution of honours.

In Shona traditional society no honours are awarded for achievement, successful ventures or services to the community. There is no public recognition of services rendered. It is preferred that all people should be the same, enjoy the same privileges and share the pleasures of nature. It is believed that to become very rich would lead to boastfulness and pride as well as giving a person unfair advantage over his fellow men, and so if a man is a little more fortunate than his neighbours he never boasts about it. I am sure that the most potent reason for this is the fear that by so doing he will attract the attentions of someone with a jealous heart, such as a witch, who will not hesitate to procure evil medicines to remove his good fortune. He cannot even be sure of his own flesh and blood, for even relations and good friends may become jealous and invoke witchcraft in order to bring about a levelling in their fortunes.

A FRIENDLY DISPOSITION

I have noticed when visiting a village how pleasant, quiet and cheerful the women are. They are not morose or depressed and whatever duties they perform they do readily. Although leisurely, their movements are not lazy and they do not show a dissatisfaction with their lot. Nothing is performed sullenly, and rudeness or a sense of superiority is never shown. This display of pleasure and contentment combined with a gentleness, quietness and lack of tension applies to men and boys as well. I have often thought about their serene contentment and I think it is cultivated because a sullen, unhappy, sour and unfriendly personality is linked with the witch. A person who grumbles, finds fault with others and complains about his lot, is not considered unhappy but associated with evil, and therefore with danger, and thus is readily suspected of practising witchcraft. Therefore no woman can afford to display these unpleasant traits.

The Shona would probably be the most happy and con-

tented of people in his traditional environment, prepared
to put up with almost any hardship if he were not afraid of
the witch.

SHARING

A child is never permitted to eat alone and quickly learns
as a matter of course that food is to be shared. Sharing of
food is never an occasion for which gratitude is expected, but
is the natural course of events.[1]

This habit of sharing food is intimately associated with the
entire mode of African traditional life, but has already been
undermined by new and modern influences which stress
virtues such as thrift, good husbandry and preparation for
a rainy day. These all tend to restrict the sharing of food and
are in direct oppostion to the normal pattern of life in Africa.
In fact these virtues can easily become vices, if transplanted
into a culture that has not at the same time been modified
to receive them.

This idea of sharing is described by Munday[2] who writes:
'The family forms an economic group, the father and sons-
in-law work together in a group, the mother and her daughters too, work together as a group. Working in these close
family groups the food was grown, the bark cloth made, the
meals prepared, houses built, iron was smelted and worked
and all the hundred and one small tasks of daily life were
performed. Granted a great forbearance in the elders, little
tact or skill in getting on with one's fellowman was needed
in such a group of closely related persons, where each knew
perfectly well his or her place. No individual could become
very rich because not only was the produce of such a family
group shared amongst its members, but also with any other
group of the same clan, which might be in want. The great
mutual responsibility between members of a clan is called
in lala ukututansyana (to pay one another's fines); it is the
responsibility of every member of a clan for the liabilities
of every other member. In actual fact such responsibility is
not usually recognized beyond three or four degrees of

[1] Howman, R. *Native Affairs Department Annual* (1942), *20, 3.*
[2] Munday, J. T. *Native Affairs Department Annual* (1942), 25. Gelfand, M. *Man.*
(1962), *62*, 114. (Correspondence.)

relationship, within these limits it is almost limitless.' Even if a man is guilty of an offence the family still bear the responsibility of his guilt. Lending a hand to any of the group in paying a fine is known as *ripira mhosva* and is still very strong among the Shona.

It is hard to assess the results of such a system on the individual character. It certainly leads to habits of open-handed generosity within the group. A sick or incapable clan member is certain of support. There are no widows and orphans in such a social organization. But it should be remembered that, good as the system is, it only works within the clan—indeed only within an extended family group. A sufferer can expect no help or mercy from those outside the clan. On the debit side, too, is the fact that the go-ahead man has no incentive to work hard or intelligently in order to amass possessions as he is expected to share them with the family circle.

In traditional society where the wealth lies in the family group and is administered by the father, it follows that if any one of the kin gets into difficulties, his obligations will be met through the family resources. A European knows, or should know, that he has his own way to make in this world and that what he reaps depends largely on what he sows. It is true he may be in the fortunate position of having a father or some other relative in the background who will help him in the ultimate issue. But he can never take this for granted. The African, reared in his traditional environment, will never be let down by his extended family group; the African in town with less binding family ties and a false feeling of security in his own ability may forget this and find himself in debt. He needs help from his family, but this is not always at hand, and in desperation he is driven to stealing. Yet I have found that even the urban African, permanently or semi-permanently resident in a city, is often helped by his rural brethren should the need arise.

At this point the subject of charity could usefully be mentioned as it is linked in some ways with the ability to share.

CHARITY

In traditional Shona society there are no charitable institutions or organizations to help people in distress; this is a contrast to Western society where these bodies came into existence centuries ago. In the Christian religion great stress is placed on charity. A good person is expected to give to the poor, the sick and lame outside his own family. It is impossible to number the multitude of organizations and institutions depending on charity. This idea of charity is foreign to the Shona and he is often accused of lack of sympathy with those less fortunate, but this is not true. The real reason for the lack of charity in his traditional society is that all people are on an equal footing and there is little material difference between the families. Each family in its small village is limited for space and lives on what it can grow, make or save. Theirs is a subsistence living and there are no rich people as we know them. A man cannot buy up land from others nor can he acquire extensive grazing-rights. There are, of course, certain differences between families, depending on their industriousness and on other factors. If a man and his wives are hard-working and careful they will have more food in their granaries, more clothes, hoes and other simple necessities, but that is all and, as mentioned previously, it is shared among all the members of that kinship group. Their position is not very different from that of their less industrious neighbours. Even a chief is not much better off than anyone else, and I have been struck by the simple way in which he lives, very similar to the rest of the tribe.

Munday (1942) describing the Lala people in Northern Rhodesia east of Broken Hill, observed that everyone in the village belongs to the same little group of relations and rarely consists of more than twenty men. The family forms an economic group, the father and sons-in-law work together as one, the mother and daughters labour as a unit. In this way the food is grown, and bark cloth made. Perhaps with his many children the African feels secure, knowing that he need not fear as long as his family unit remains large and intact. He will never want. He is not an individual working for himself; his security is the family. Therefore he needs no outside help. No charitable bodies are necessary in this social system which ensures that all have the same opportunity and all are of one company. It is not that the African is uncharitable, but that the social structure of his life does away with the need for organized charity.

TO THE END

Possibly related to the ability to 'stall', and being of a friendly disposition, is the attribute which I have termed 'To the End', which is designed to display the utmost interest in other members of the family or friends, a desire to please or an attempt to avoid any inference of greed.

At a ceremony at which beer is served the man organizing the affair makes sure that all the beer brewed is consumed. Very little is ever left. It has to be enjoyed by all and everyone must be satisfied. All the meat from a beast killed at a ritual sacrifice is eaten or given away to special dignitaries during the ceremony. None must be kept or the spirit will be offended.

When the men eat at the *dare* or the women in their huts, they must eat until they are satisfied. It is impolite to refuse. Yet the Shona does not countenance greed or the taking away of a portion that belongs to someone else.

The African's smile of pleasure is wholehearted and his sorrow complete. He gives vent to his feelings without holding back. Yet he does not lack restraint or self-control. But when there is need to express his feelings he displays little restraint. If pleasure is to be shown or if the occasion merits sorrow, the appropriate feeling is written all over his face. He does not dissemble. It is easy to tell whether he is pleased or angered. With the European it is often said, that the better he is schooled the more difficult it is to know his feelings or innermost thoughts. With the Shona there is no difficulty in understanding his reactions.

9   *Language and Culture*

(*by the* Rev. Father M. Hannan, S.J.)

'I am sorry to have to do so, but I must confess that I find this people completely lacking in culture.' This remark about the Shona was made by a well-disposed observer. His contact with the Shona was somewhat wider than the usual one of master and servant: he had observed the people with sympathy and he had read widely. But, alas, he did not know their language!

If one uses the word culture with one meaning, then any people having a permanent form of social organization must be said to have its own culture. In another context, culture is taken as meaning a developed art. But there is still a third meaning of the word; a person, or a people, is said to be cultured if he or it has an appreciation of values that are other than the merely material or useful. No one could deny that the Shona have their own culture, using the word in the way in which the ethnologists of, let us say, the Kulturkreise school use it. Few would credit the Shona with having developed pictorial art. But he would be a rash man who denies that the Shona have an appreciation of values other than the merely material and useful.

There are 'nature's gentlemen' among all peoples, and the contention that the Shona have culture means more than just that there are nature's gentlemen among the Shona as among other peoples. These few paragraphs are not being written with the intention of proving to anyone that the Shona have culture; on the contrary, it is the writer's conviction that they have, and the aim of these few paragraphs is simply to call attention to the way in which the language of

102

the Shona shows them to have an appreciation of values that are other than the merely material or useful.

Gestures are a part of language, and though a nod may mean assent to speakers of some languages, it also means denial to speakers of other languages. There is, however, one gesture that is used synonymously by the speakers of most languages. The hand is held, with the palm facing down, and is raised or lowered by the speaker in order to indicate his estimate of the height or tallness of something. The Shona speaker uses this gesture, too, but he uses it only when he is indicating the height of something that grows; maize in a field, for example. When he wishes to indicate the height of a calf, the hand is held with the palm turned inwards and with the little finger nearest to the ground. But the gesture for showing the height of a human being is different; to indicate this the arm is bent at the elbow, and the hand is bent at the wrist, the palm facing down. Is it far-fetched to read a whole philosophy behind this use of three different gestures, when the reference is to different kinds of living things? There are sure to be those who would tell us that a Shona could not refer to a child's height by holding his hand out with the palm facing down, because the gestures might be interpreted as a wish that the child should not grow. Similarly, he could not indicate the height of a child with the palm facing inwards, because this might be interpreted as a wish on his part that the child should grow broader rather than taller. For my part I am content to accept the fact, that there are three different kinds of gestures, as suggestive that in Shona thought vegetative, animal and human life are conceived of as essentially different.

There is, as far as I know, no word in Shona for vegetative life or for animal life, but there is an abstract word *Umunhu* which we might translate as 'human nature'. Coming from the same root is the word *unhu*. It is heard in such sentences as: *Musikana uyo haana unhu*—that girl lacks the modesty a Shona girl should have. *Murume uyo ano unhu*—that man has those qualities of self-control, co-operativeness and respect for the elders that a Shona man is expected to have. These are only two examples of the use of the word, but they are enough to suggest that *unhu* is the Shona word for what we are talking about, for an appreciation of values that are more than the merely material or useful. Just as mere possession of a book does not make anyone the master of its contents, so the fact that there is a Shona word for culture is no more than another probability that the Shona have culture. It will be found that there are very many such probabilities and that they all point to the same conclusion.

There is a French verb *tutoyer*, with the meaning of 'being on familiar terms', to which chiShona has the equivalent *kunemana*. But chiShona also has a whole system of tonal and grammatical inflexions to express respect and reverence. There is not the space here in which to give even an outline of what some grammarians call the plural of respect. It might be sufficient to say that the use of honorifics in chiShona is, by itself, evidence of a behaviour pattern of respect for elders that is similar to that behaviour pattern of respect for women that is the hallmark of a European man of culture. The Shona who has no respect for his elders is regarded by his fellows as a barbarian, as lacking in culture.

One set of gestures, one word and one grammatical characteristic of the language of the Shona have been instanced as indications that the Shona are a people with culture. What evidence does Shona literature afford us? Of the three main kinds of oral literature—ritual songs and utterances, proverbs and folk-tales—there is space to refer, and that very briefly, to only the last two.

There is a fairly large volume to be written which will contain the many hundreds of Shona proverbs that are in daily use. This should be followed by several volumes of interpretation of the proverbs. It is obvious, then, that in this short space all that I can do is to point out that one who has not made a study of the proverbs cannot honestly say that he has searched for signs of culture and found none. We can take the first proverbs that come to mind as showing an appreciation of values that are more than merely material,

A son-in-law has come to tell his father-in-law something. Note the characteristic posture with the head turned away. (see page 62.)

At a *hoka* ceremony in the Nyondoro reserve. Friends and neighbours have come on the day to help the owner of the land to weed. (see page 48.)

At a ritual ceremony. Observe how the female and male position their hands while clapping. (see page 63.)

as an instance of what would be found if a serious study of the proverbs were made.

Chawawana idya nehama, mutorwa anokanganwa: It is with a relative that you should share what falls to you, a fellow villager who is not kin will forget. This is one of the many proverbs that speak of one or other aspect of family solidarity. But there is a higher loyalty than that to kin, as is expressed in the proverb: *kumuẕinda washe hakuna woko:* at the chief's court there is no favourite (not even a relative). In other words, justice is valued even higher than kinship. A third proverb, in somewhat the same context, says, *murau ndishe:* law is the chief. In other words, right conduct is even more absolute than the will of a chief.

If one examines Shona folk-tales, looking for traces of culture, it will be easy to be led astray by the facile suggestion that since the folk-tales make a hero out of a cunning hare they cannot yield evidence of culture, of the appreciation of values other than the merely material and useful. Again, the field of the *ngano* is so wide and my space here is so short that I can only take the first example that comes to mind and offer it as one single instance out of very many.

The story goes that Hare invited the Baboon family to his village for a friendly meal. In the morning of the day of the party, Hare instructed his wife to burn the grass surrounding their village. A full and appetizing meal was prepared and the guests arrived on time. Baboon and his family felt their mouths watering in anticipation. as they smelt the delicious odours coming from the kitchen. However, Hare told his guests that there was one thing he could not do and that was to sit down to a meal with people who had dirty hands. 'It is a mere formality, of course, but would you mind showing me your hands?' he said. As he knew quite well, Baboon and his family had come through recently burnt grass and their hands were blackened with soot. 'Well, really!' said Hare, 'I did not expect this from you, Mr. Baboon. Please take your family down to the stream and wash their hands. The wife and I will not wait for you, so hurry back.' To cut the story short, each time Baboon and

8

his family came back from washing in the stream they passed through the burnt grass and arrived with dirty hands and were sent back to the stream, until Hare and his family had finished off all the food.

A few days later, Hare was, perhaps, slightly surprised to receive an invitation from Baboon to make a return visit to his home and share a simple meal. On the day, and at the time, Hare arrived with his family at the village of Mr. Baboon. Their nostrils were assailed by mouth-watering smells of cooking delicacies. Hare was somewhat perplexed to see Mrs. Baboon setting the table high up in a tree. You can appreciate his chagrin when his host said to him: 'I'm sorry old chap, but I have a thing, too, about eating. You don't like eating with people who have dirty hands; I don't like eating on the ground. Come up and join us.'

10   *The Spiritual Concept*

Father Placide Tempels, an authority on the Baluba in the Congo, has of recent years published his hypothesis of Bantu philosophy, and it is largely due to him that an enlightened outlook on the African spiritual culture has come into being. Tempels's *Bantu Philosophy*[1] is the most quoted work of its kind. He defines his metaphysical approach as the 'Philosophy of Force' and claims that it is a theory of life and provides a rational explanation of African behaviour. This philosophy of force strictly governs the whole of Bantu life. His hypothesis incorporates three main laws:

1. Man (living or deceased) can develop, reinforce or diminish the being of another man. Such vital influence is possible from man to man: it is indeed necessarily effective as between the progenitor—a superior vital force—and his progeny—an inferior force.

2. The vital human force can directly influence inferior force-beings (animal, vegetable or mineral) in their being itself.

3. A rational being (spirit, manes or living) can act indirectly upon another rational being by communicating his vital influence to an inferior force (animal, vegetable or mineral) through the intermediary of which it influences the rational being. This influence will also have the character of a necessarily effective action, save only when the object is inherently the superior force, or is reinforced by the influence of some third party, or preserves himself by recourse to inferior forces exceeding those which his enemy is employing.

---

[1] Tempels, P. *Bantu Philosophy* (1952). Collection *Presence Africaine*, Paris.

'Bantu Behaviour', says Tempels, 'is centred in a single value: vital force.' Where does this force come from? 'When they try to get away from metaphors and periphrases, the Bantu speak of God himself as "the Strong One", he who possesses force in himself. He is also the source of the force of every creature.' It is from God that this vital force is passed on to the spirits, the dead and the intermediaries to whom the Bantu pray.

Jan-heinz[2] has developed further the philosophy of Tempels on the African religion, supporting his arguments on work done in this field by Marcel Griaule, who studied the people in the great bend of the Niger; Germaine Dietherlen, who investigated the religion of the Bambara of Central Africa, and of Alexis Kagame, himself a Bantu, who has special knowledge of the Africans living in the Ruanda. Basically the study is an extension or further development of Tempels's hypothesis. Everything in nature or the four basic concepts such as human being (*muntu*), thing (*kintu*), place and time (*hantu*) and modality (*kuntu*) must be conceived not as mere substances but as possessing a force or a being itself which he terms *Ntu*. *Ntu* is the universal force, the *being*, the cosmic universal force, *Ntu* is the quality of being. Perhaps one might regard *Ntu* as the character which distinguishes one thing from another. And how is life or being alive explained? Firstly there is *buzima* or biological life. This belongs to the category *kuntu* or of way or manner and starts when an animal shadow unites with a body. After death the shadow disappears and the body is lost. Nothing remains of the body of an animal after death. But in the production of a human being, possessed of intelligence, there is another force, called *nommo*, which unites with the *buzima* (biological life = union of body and animal shadow) to produce a new principle or power called *magara* or spiritual life. *Nommo* is the driving power, or quality of intelligence possessed by *muntu*. But the word *muntu* does not only mean a human being, for it

[2] Jan-heinz, J. *Muntu—an outline of Neo-African culture* (1961). Faber & Faber, London (translated by Grene, M.). Gelfand, M. *Native Affairs Department Annual* (1965), *19*, 94.

includes both the living and the dead. When a man dies his biological life (*buʐima*) comes to an end as well as his spiritual life (*magara*), but his life force (or personality) (*nommo*) remains in the *muʐimu*—the spirit guardian—rather comparable to a human being not alive but possessed of a spiritual force which can still influence the living descendants.

Thus *muntu* has control over the other categories like *kintu* (animals and objects) by allowing this force of *nommo* to activate their being and so altering their qualities. The *muʐimu* of man is therefore a spiritual force which can influence his living descendants and in this way increase the life force of their descendants. *Magara* when present in the living can lead to happiness and contentment as well as being responsible for intelligence and living man can allow some of it to flow and strengthen the ancestral spirits through prayer, sacrifice and honour. It is the head of the family who offers the sacrifice. The dead therefore are of different strengths depending on whether there are descendants on earth to pray and make sacrifices to them.

I agree with Father Tempels that the African as I know him believes in a vital force which he owes to the Creator, but is this not the same claim one makes for any religion? Can we not say that in other religions there is the same belief? Certainly the Christian and the Jew believe in such a spiritual force, and I would here make the plea that the vital force which the African believes in is similar only in certain respects to what the Christian understands. This vital force, however, constitutes the pillar or foundation of Christianity and it cannot be said to be a feature only of the religion of the African.

This vital force, derived from God, permeates everyone and everything in Nature. 'Every African', says Tempels, 'seeks this vital force above all else.' It is in the interpretation and application of this force by the African however that disagreement may occur. Does the way the African believes in the force or power of good tie in with what the Christian accepts? Is the way the Spirit force renders its effects similar to that of the Christian God? Is the African's doctrine different even if the African accepts the presence of God? The Christian looks directly to God for this force, but the African in my experience turns to God only in an indirect way. He places immediate and great reliance on his spiritual hierarchy. These spirits, good and bad, have not only tremendous power and influence but are also endowed with particular functions. When faced with a crisis the Shona turn not to God in the first instance but to a particular group of spirits depending on their spiritual functions. Thus they seek this power or force from the tribal spirits (*mhondoro*) when they are in the throes of a drought; from their ancestral spirits (*vadzimu*) when it is a personal matter concerning their individual families. The man who owes his special talent for hunting or doctoring to an alien spirit (*shave*) prays to this spirit should he find that the special talent has forsaken him. With very few exceptions do the Shona think in terms of a personal and Almighty God, although I will allow that the Shona admit that ultimately all power and the force which Tempels stresses emanates from Him. In a somewhat similar way the Shona looks upon the evil spirit of the witch as a variety of *shave* which can possess man. Here then certain individuals are endowed with the powers of evil, powers not known to the ancestral spirits and not linked with any other spiritual form other than the spirit or *shave* of evil which is inherited and passed on from parent to child. The ancestral spirits are called upon to protect the living members of the family against the intrusion of their homes by witches.

Father Tempels goes further in maintaining that not only do the Africans see this vital force emanating from God and extending into the spiritual world but into everything which surrounds him. The Shona do appreciate that life exists in plants and trees and are ready to believe even that their ancestral spirits may at times reside in trees. It is everywhere around him. The vital spirit is all over and is part of nature. But is this really African in concept, for the Christian feels, too, that nature—the force of life—is everywhere! If Father Tempels means that the Bantu believe that inanimate

objects possess a soul, then I disagree. I am quite certain
that the Shona do not accept this. It is not part of their belief
that inanimate objects possess a soul. My contact with the
Shona convinces me that they are not animists. They do not
pray to animals. The fact that the Shona remember an
ancestral spirit (spirit elder) by dedicating or sacrificing a
bull or beast to the spirit so that it may be remembered is
not to be associated with prayers being made to the actual
bull. When the animal is reserved in honour of the spirit
of the family, prayers are made next to the animal; these
are directed to the spirit itself. The same prayer is made when
any gift or offering is made to the spirit. In a rather similar
way the witch employs his familiars, but prayers are never
made to them by those who belong to this cult. When Father
Tempels argues that the gifted African attributes any talent
displayed by him to this vital force I can again detect the
philosophy of the Christian in this, for Tempels believes that
he is permanently possessed or endowed with it. But the
Shona do not share this view in the same way as Tempels
implies. There is a subtle difference, for while the *shave*
or spirit conferring the particular talent on the individual can
be said to be part of the vital force, the Shona claim that
this talented spirit periodically possesses its selected host.

Without such spiritual reinforcement (and in this context
I would agree with Father Tempels in the existence of a
vital force) the individual cannot operate his talent. In order
that he might take advantage of it and utilize it he must
carry out a prescribed ritual, for unless he does so he will not
be able to divine, engage in a successful hunt or enjoy a
dance in the way he otherwise would. Failure to respect the
wishes of his *shave* reduces him to the level of the average or
ordinary man. In his ordinary daily routine whether in his
fields or when tending to his cattle, he is like any other
man, but when he wishes to utilize his special gift such as
hunting, he must always undergo a special ritual so that
his *shave* may enter him. In this state of possession he can
make use of the talent as long as he deems it necessary. When
it is no longer needed the spirit leaves him and he becomes

reduced once again to an ordinary being.

Father Tempels quite rightly claims, in my opinion, that a knowledge of the African's religion will give one a better understanding of his behaviour. To quote his own words, 'Bantu behaviour: It is centred in a single value: vital force.' The Bantu, he states, seeks, yearns for a supply of this force. 'Force,' he says, 'the potent life, vital energy are the object of prayers and invocations to God, to the spirits and to the dead, as well as of all that is usually called magic, sorcery or magical remedies. The Bantu will tell you that they go to a diviner to learn the words of life, so that he can teach them the way of making life stronger. In every Bantu language it is easy to recognize the words or phrases denoting a force which is not used in an exclusively bodily sense, but in the sense of the integrity of our whole being.' Again Father Tempels writes: 'In calling upon God, the spirits, or the ancestral spirits, the heathen ask above all "Give me force".' I find it difficult as a doctor to accept this, because if the Shona were seeking such strength, vitality or zest in life in order to live 'strongly', I find little evidence of it in the Shona's behaviour. It is quite true one of the common Shona greetings is *'Wakasimba bere?'* (Are you strong?), but I interpret this as meaning that the inquirer hopes that his friend is well, just as when a Jew toasts another, he invariably adds as he raises the glass, 'to life'.

I am struck more with the pleasant, quiet, respectful attitude of child and adult. On the many occasions I have sat with Africans in their villages I have repeatedly noticed the silent and extremely fine behaviour of the children, so different from the boisterousness and vivaciousness of the European, a vitality quite different from the sedate yet thoughtful African child.

Over the years I have found that the output or productive capacity of the Shona can be regarded as being normal unless they are afflicted by tropical ailments. They tend to be quiet except when there are special occasions, but even when they are gathered together as at a dance, the onlookers are often composed and more silent than at a similar European function.

I must confess that as the Shona live in a country where malaria and bilharziasis are endemic, and as good food is not generally plentiful, such quiet and calm which I describe could be attributed to the effects of chronic disease. It is accepted in medicine for instance that a child or adult who harbours the bilharzial parasites is tired and lacks interest. And what must never be forgotten is that almost all the population living under traditional conditions are affected each to a greater or lesser extent by one or more of these parasitic disorders or from malnutrition. However, I have observed Africans who are free from these diseases— nurses, orderlies, messengers and many others who stay in towns—and again in them I detect the same calm, the same poise and composure, the same attributes which are linked with a well-behaved person. I am not struck by an undue vivacity or an unusual vitality. And it is on this point of expression of vitality as reflected in the African's behaviour that I would differ from Tempels.

Father Tempels, in support of his argument, uses as an example the African who goes to the diviner to learn whether or not he is going to live. But is this not also the same motive of the European when he consults his medical adviser? The reasons for seeking medical aid are precisely the same in the two races.

But there is another 'force' or influence which greatly affects the behaviour of the African. One, as just mentioned, is the way the religious tenets of God are interpreted by the people and I have indicated that the African's belief in the vital force does not reflect itself in the way or mode in which he conducts his life. The other belief which I feel Tempels has not adequately dealt with is the 'Power of Evil' which the Bantu believe exists in certain people, a force which like the 'Creative Force', is passed on to the kin, a power so prevalent that every person must be on guard against it. It is incumbent on every person to be at peace with the ancestral spirits which will protect them against the intrusions of the witch. The witch is ever jealous, envious, and anyone who is rich, boastful, proud or successful, quarrels and is bound to attract the attention of the witch who will inflict untold suffering, misery and death upon that fortunate individual. Does this force of evil come from the Creator? What does the African think about this terrible force—without which Man would be ever happy and fortunate? I have asked my Shona this and I believe they do not link this force of evil with the Creator or God, but believe that it arose countless generations before in the group or clan of evil people, and the evil spirit, like the *shave* or *mudzimu*, has been handed down in the families. Belief by the African in the cult of evil accounts for—as much as any factor—the great tendency to conform. Belief in ancestral spirits also accounts, just as acceptance of the 'Force of Evil', for conformity among the Bantu. Belief in this vital force tends to force individuals to behave in a similar manner to others in this society. It does not tend to spur on the society as Father Tempels maintains.

The Shona are clear when they state that the *vadzimu* are their protectors who possess the power of preventing evil from entering their midst, almost in the rule or guise of a policeman. These spirits are on guard, so to speak, around and in the midst of their living quarters. In this way the witch can never enter their homes and villages. Therefore in order to keep well and happy the family must remember and respect the *vadzimu*. Further, the Shona believe that the *vadzimu*, when annoyed, bring sickness and even death upon the individuals of the guilty family by withdrawing this particular vital protection and so permitting the evil influence to enter. In many ways the *vadzimu* are spirits who are more feared and respected than loved. The awe of the Shona towards their *vadzimu* is very similar to that of the Jew to God. Sin and transgression, remembered even unto the third and fourth generation, will invoke the wrath of the Almighty. It is this fear of the power of the *vadzimu* which has the opposite effect of spurring on the individual. He is, rather, forced to conform, not to change, and to live in the same way as his father and forefathers before him. The cult of ancestors tends to create a static society. Thus we meet two important forces which account for the desire by the African to conform; the first is fear of the ancestral spirits (*vadzimu*) and the second the fear of the evil spirits in certain people (*uroyi*). In this way through these two forces, the powerful vital force of God, the Creator, is counteracted.

Father Tempels implies that man (living or dead) can develop, reinforce or demolish the being of another man and that such vital influence is possible from man to man. The Shona do not think of their *vadzimu* as being capable of increasing the talents or the qualities with which every individual is endowed. The trait which each individual possesses, be it healing, skill, ability to work and cook, is that which the Creator (*Mwari*) has bestowed on one. They cannot transfer to, or enhance any quality in, an individual. They can, however, remove their protective ability and so allow enemies to gain an entrance to an individual's body and so weaken him.

The *vadzimu* cannot create power—this is solely what man owes to his Creator (*Mwari*). Can the Shona tribal spirits (*mhondoro*) make rain? Are they creative? They cannot bring rain by their own creation but, as they are intermediaries between man and the Creator, they are able to bring their influences to bear on Him. However, in almost all my investigations as to the cause of a drought, whether it was to the far north or south of Mashonaland, the reason given for it has been that the tribal spirit was annoyed for one or other reason. It may have been that a man committed incest, or one of the tribesmen worked on the holy day of rest, or the spirit was angry because the tribesmen spoke to me—a white man—about the customs of the people and because of these offences, he withheld the rain. The spirit has the power to stop something already in existence just as the *vadzimu* could interfere with the health already bestowed on the individual. Indeed the tribal spirit cannot only stop the rain, but it can as an intermediary with the Creator even refuse to stop it once it has come and so cause floods and ruination of the fields. In other words it would seem that the tribal spirit can interfere with the fall of rain although it cannot actively make or create it.

It may be argued that the *mudzimu* or the *shave* spirit can increase the talent or ability of the individual. I must admit that at first sight it would effect this by conferring on the selected person an increase of the vital force. The Shona think that the *mudzimu* or *shave* possesses an individual and it is during this state of possession that his particular talent is emphasized. The *mudzimu* or *shave* spirit is able to increase his powers of divination only so long as his *mudzimu* is within him. When the spirit leaves him as it must after several or more hours, that individual assumes his normal state once again.

To the Shona God is more in the nature of the very Great Spirit, the Creator of all life who does not concern Himself with every item or problem of a person's life—he is far removed and his help is not invoked in the vast majority of instances. For almost every problem or crisis the lesser spirits are prayed to and invoked for their help in solving the difficulty. There is perhaps one exception in that the Vakaranga—a large section of the Shona people concentrated around Fort Victoria—approach *Mlimo* (God) on special although rare occasions. However, for practical purposes the method of prayer is exactly the same as with the other Shona tribes, but when there is a special problem which cannot be resolved by the ordinary deities, a delegation of tribesmen is sent to a special rock or shrine in the Matopo Hills, near Bulawayo, where an oracle exists. On sitting down near the opening to a cave a voice is heard—the voice of *Mlimo*, we are told, and the voice provides an explanation in Shona to the particular question. This spirit is prayed to and appealed to in the same way as the lesser spirits by giving it presents of consecrated beer to drink and snuff to enjoy. I have elaborated this point in order to point out that I find I cannot agree with Father Tempels when he uses the word God for the Shona who, while they admit the presence of the Creator, invariably approach their ancestral and tribal spirits for comfort and help in the first instance.

A young man about to speak to the woman who is seated on the ground. He is half kneeling and can be seen to be clapping his hands lengthwise in typical male fashion. The husband of the woman claps his hands out of respect to the visitor. (see page 63.)

A father hands over a plate to his daughter, who receives it in the kneeling position. Kandeya reserve, northern Mashonaland.) (see page 68.)

A Shona woman demonstrates the traditional way she would approach husband or senior man. (see page 64.)

As she places the food down, the men acknowledge it with the customary clapping. (see page 68.)

Women in a dance in the Mount Darwin district of northern Mashonaland. (see page 97.)

A group of African girls about an evening fire in a village. Note their
beautiful smiles. (Kandeya reserve, 1960.) (see page 101.)

Shona men gathered at a beer drink. (see page 74.)

The Shona have a spiritual faith which in its basic principles has much that the monotheist believes. On the other hand there are very clear differences, the most striking being that the religion in contributing to conformity lacks the dynamism of Christianity. All members of the clans are to be alike, none richer than his fellow man in material things, although there are accepted differences in the social status in the kin group. But the religion does not encourage differences which would affect the material status of a person. All are to possess more or less the same, and all are to enjoy the material benefits of life equally. Every man and woman must follow the examples set by their grandparents or departed parents, on this earth. If a person does not do what one's beloved elders did before him, all will not be well. Should this individual show greed and stray away from the course of life his parents practised, nothing but trouble will follow. I have previously spoken of this feature of Shona behaviour as compulsory uniformity. This is, in my opinion, the most outstanding feature of African life—viz. to be like everyone else, to be just normal.

I have already shown how the talent conferred on the host or medium by the *shave* spirit is the basis for the display of any outstanding ability or brilliance exhibited by an individual. Every person is born equal with the same ability as everyone else, making allowances for slight variations from the mean. Omit to carry out the ritual prescriptions of the particular *shave* and the talent will leave the selected person and he becomes just like any other individual.

We notice this urge—almost amounting to an obsession —for conformity in almost monotonous regularity in African clothes, living quarters, utensils and so forth. Enter any Shona village in a tribal area and then compare it with another in that area—one is forcibly struck by the sameness throughout. They do not seem to have developed any fashion, mode of dress or of living. It is all the same and this uniformity in the society has been mistakenly attributed by outsiders and observers to the fact that the African is incompetent, backward, and unambitious. It means that the

9

individual has to live the life of his ancestors.

In this philosophy of forces, Tempels explains the human motivations of all Bantu customs. It lays down standards in accordance with which the personality of the individual shall remain unaltered or allowed to develop. Some of the standards, Tempels states, allow the individual to develop further because of the vital force, but my contention is that no development is permitted beyond the norm in so far as conduct is concerned. According to Father Tempels, the Bantu who is endowed with a special ability can develop his interests provided these lie within his prescribed standards or norms. I have found that the Shona has not encouraged the full development of the individual's talent in matters vital to the welfare of the clan. For instance, Shona philosophy has discouraged the African from devising ways of storing water so that in the event of a drought the community can be saved. The Shona, it will be argued, has changed from millet to maize but by so doing no basic alterations have taken place in their spiritual life by interfering with the course of nature. There is to be no evolution, no change from the bare standards which would ensure a normal mode of existence. The aim and object of a happy existence is to live at peace with nature, to utilize the essentials which ensure a reasonable standard of comfort. There is no need, for instance, to have spring mattresses to sleep on for nothing can go wrong if the individual sleeps on a reed mat on the ground. It is much safer, more reliable to live simply—which after all is only a matter of becoming accustomed to it. This approach has been well tried, and, as far as he can see, it serves the purpose well.

In Father Tempels's analysis one can detect something of the Bergsonian philosophy—indeed the dynamism which is so typical of Christianity. It is here that I differ from him. The Shona faith ensures—and this probably also applies to that of all the Southern Bantu—conformity, quite the reverse of Christianity.

11   *Normal Behaviour and Attributes*

In this chapter I propose to discuss the features of African behaviour that have impressed me most. Behaviour is a term which covers a great deal, but a study of a person's conduct gives a good idea of his make-up and character. How does an African behave when faced with a problem? Are his actions dictated by his religious beliefs or by the fear of witchcraft? What does he try to achieve, and what does he avoid? How does the African treat his children, his wife, his parents, his elders, his friends and even strangers? What is his attitude to crime, robbery or revengeful acts? Does he control his emotions in a difficult situation? Is he able to keep his temper? Is he ready to help others and is he hard-working? Perhaps if we can answer these questions we may come nearer to an appreciation of his make-up. In earlier pages I have already attempted to deal with many of these questions. We should also inquire into the legal machinery that operates in traditional society to ensure that the people behave correctly.

The Shona tends to be normal in behaviour. He treasures the same virtues as the European. He despises the person who is untruthful and tells lies. *Mharadzi* is the name given to one who makes untrue statements and who has a bad character. The *mharadzi* spreads lies and rumours about others in the village and harms them. He may steal and is considered likely to plant poisons in the path of someone else. He is apt to become involved in arguments with the headman of the village. Sooner or later people become suspicious of him and he has to leave. Even his blood relations turn against him and unite to drive him away. In short, the *mharadzi* is, in some ways, likened to a witch.

On the other hand honesty (*kuvimbisika*) is an important quality. The child is constantly reminded by his parents that it is wrong to tell lies and that he must always tell the truth, not only to his relatives, but to friends and acquaintances. There is no justification for telling lies. Formerly whenever a child told a lie he was punished by having hot, roasted peanuts put under his clothes next to his body. The same happened if he took something from the house without permission or helped himself from a pot of relish left by his mother.

Kindness (*mwoyochena*) is greatly appreciated and this quality is highly valued. From an early age parents stress this virtue and praise its exercise.

Love (*rudo*) is one of the characteristics displayed by the Shona. It is very evident between parents and their children. The cult of ancestral spirits, of the grandfather and grandmother, aims at uniting and cementing the family and promoting love and affection between kin. The close association between blood relations is one of the most important features of the Shona family unit.

Jealousy is a trait greatly disapproved of by the Shona. This is met with in both sexes and exists as much among Africans as among Europeans. Success is likely to arouse envy in others. Children are warned about this bad trait and taught that a person with this fault is similar to a witch.

Greediness is another bad quality much disliked as it is against public interests for one person to eat more than his share. A person is expected to enjoy his full share, but to eat anything above this is considered greedy and antisocial. Any child who is greedy and inconsiderate to others is given a beating by his mother. On the other hand if a person is given food it is correct for him to show his appreciation of it and to eat it all, even if it is more than he really requires. By not accepting what he is offered he may be thought rude. So when an African accepts food after he is already satisfied, it is not a sign of greed but of appreciation. He need not fear that he will be accused of greed as long as no one else goes short as a result.

Howman,[1] who has paid special attention to the virtues and qualities of the Shona, confirms that such words as hatred (*ruvengo*), jealousy (*godo*), evil spreading and scandal (*kutaura makuhwa*) are employed by the Shona to describe the characteristics of the witch (*muroyi*). Anyone who falls ill or suffers misfortune is likely to interpret his distress in terms of the venting on him of those feelings of enmity which he knows someone else feels for him.

Possibly linked with the good attributes of behaviour is the Shona's attitude towards beauty. On many occasions I have pointed out a magnificent view when in the company of an African—the grandeur of a range of hills, the beauty of a distant valley, the colour of autumn leaves perhaps. But whenever I expected my companion to express admiration of something lovely in nature I have been disappointed. At most I have had a nod of agreement or an indifferent reply to my exclamation, one of politeness rather than of enjoyment. On the other hand I cannot recall an African remarking on an ugly object or an unpleasant scene.

Flowers are not cultivated in a traditional African village. There is no attempt to surround a house with a lovely garden, nor are wild flowers ever picked and brought into the home to beautify it. Nor is the home itself adorned. There are no pictures on the walls, no objects placed around to beautify its interior. All houses are built the same with the same idea of utility. Not even the household pots so highly prized by the women or the mats woven by the men are fashioned for the sake of beauty. They are all the same. No one strives to create something to reflect his own artistic individuality.

I am not trying to infer that an African does not appreciate beauty for I am sure he does, but, I think, his conception of beauty is not a purely physical sense but more a metaphysical one that goes deeper than that of the average European. I have frequently asked Africans from widely different parts of Mashonaland what a young man looks for when he selects his wife. Is his marriage based on love or a pure physical

[1] Howman, R. *Native Affairs Department Annual* (1948), 25, 7.

attraction and is he influenced in any way by these attributes? Invariably I have been assured that the young couple only marry if they are satisfied they will live happily together. I then ask, 'What do you look for in a girl?' It is true that he is first attracted by her looks, her face and figure, but thereafter the emphasis is always on a pleasant character, a happy disposition, good behaviour and readiness to work in her home. Last but not least he must make sure that her family has a good reputation and is free of the taint of witchcraft. He stresses her character above all else. Therefore, as I see it, the African looks for virtues and thus beauty in a deeper metaphysical sense than the European. He gives beauty a different meaning. To him outward appearances do not matter as much. Perhaps beauty and ugliness in the physical sense have no special meaning to him. All people are essentially the same in appearance and what matters is their characters. In this the African has probably something to teach the Western world. There is no doubt that there is a wide difference between the two races in the expression of love or affection. The traditional African does not kiss. Lovers do not kiss one another and a parent does not kiss his child. Yet this act is almost automatic in a European. The African loves in the same way without this particular physical act.

I have been puzzled for long by the extreme rarity with which an African marries a girl with the same totem. This practically never happens, although in a tribal area the vast majority of children and unmarried young adults must necessarily be of the same totem. In European towns love affairs continually follow contact between the two sexes living in the same neighbourhood. A boy is attracted to a girl and often without further ado the couple marries. Yet this rarely happens with the African, who takes it for granted that a girl in his village or the neighbouring one is not for him. He has learnt to control his senses. When he reaches the age of independence and is old enough to marry he visits the villages and homes of clansmen with different totems to his own until he eventually meets the woman with whom he believes he can enter into a happy union. From an early age he is taught that happiness does not depend on mere physical attraction or beauty but on character. He values honesty, kindness, good behaviour and consideration towards others and expects these virtues to be present in the partner he contemplates marrying.

Concluding Thoughts

I believe that the spiritual beliefs of the Shona tend to make them conform in behaviour and outlook. As their ancestors were good, kind and decent people, so their descendants are expected to follow their example. What is good for the father is good for the children. Everyone, no matter what his or her position in the family hierarchy, is equally a member of the family, and is given the same opportunity and scope. The cult of witchcraft also tends to force people to be pleasant, well-behaved and to conform. Thus the Shona prefers the normal man. He is not greedy nor wants to be the best or most clever in the world. His philosophy does not lead to dynamism. His religion is not dynamic because discovery and change lead to rivalry and rivalry to loss of friendship among individuals and to war between clans and nations.

Peace is best maintained by preserving the *status quo*. This is in marked contrast to Christianity, which, although it calls upon man to be content with his lot, allows scope for change and encourages progress. The difficulty is where to draw the line in change, and leading Christians are not a little concerned at the innovations being introduced by many of the scientific discoveries. In Christian Europe about 500 hundred years ago the Church was strongly resistant to change and I can quote no better example than the burning of Michael Servitus in Geneva in October 1553 because he had the audacity to suggest a different route for the blood from the heart to the lungs than that postulated by Galen and accepted as the truth by the Church. But it came to terms with scientific discovery through the tradition inherited from Thomas Aquinas in the thirteenth century and as a result the Christian could identify himself with scientific progress and change with a clear conscience. Even in the Dark and Middle Ages the Church allowed a little scope for enterprise and some avenues of thought were still open to men. With the Shona there are virtually no allowances. Conformity is the rule in all phases of conduct and behaviour as well as in ritual practices.

We must not forget that even in European societies there are very few geniuses. They are exceptional. A bright man is not a genius and strictly speaking almost all men quoted as exceptional are normal. A normal mentality is a fine attribute. Admittedly there are degrees of normality among men and women; some are more able than others, but the point I wish to stress is that the people we know are normal. From time to time we see subnormal people and we are told that in England no less than 10 to 20 per cent of children at school are mentally subnormal for one reason or another. The African is normal in mentality and physique and it is my impression that there are fewer subnormals in his society than in European circles. I think there are more normal Africans than normal Europeans. A great number of Africans are bright and intelligent, but throughout the ages, although the European genius was rare, it would seem that there have been still fewer African geniuses. A genius is liable to cause changes in his society because of a discovery he has made. There may be opposition to his newer methods, but as a rule, the innovations are accepted, even if grudgingly. It is impossible to prove my contention, but I firmly believe that a genius would not be welcomed in traditional African society. In fact, his life would be in danger and he would most certainly be driven out of his village. In this society there is no place for a man who tries to alter the course of nature and such a person is likely to be labelled a witch. In European society although he is not welcomed by his fellow men, the genius generally succeeds in making his contribution. He cannot be quietened; at all costs he must reveal his message.

Again, while I cannot prove this with actual figures, my experience shows that the mentally defective is relatively infrequent in African society. It is difficult to know how often this eventuality occurs in a community, but over many years of practice and clinical work in the paediatric wards I have noticed the comparative infrequency of mental retardation in the African in contrast to the European.

It is quite possible that not only is the African mentality more often normal than in the European, but he also seems to have a more normal body. For instance we find that almost all Africans are normal sighted. A myopic is rarely encountered among them in contrast to the European, and it would seem reasonable to argue that formerly in his society where his survival depended on trapping and killing of game, an individual with a subnormal vision would have found it more difficult to protect himself in a hostile environment. In fact, the myopic could not have been expected to fend for himself and survive. So after some generations, with the elimination by accident of individuals with poor eyesight, only children with normal eyesight are born.

I am not stating however that there have been no African geniuses. Obviously Chaka the great Zulu leader had this spark and creative power and there were others. But the point I wish to make is that while there are more geniuses in Europe, in the same way there are more mentally dull people. In Africa the trend is more towards normality and less towards the extremes on either side of it.

Professor Gluckman[1] in his book on the *Judicial Process among the Barotse* analyses the rationale behind the judgments made in their tribal courts. He has shown that in coming to judgment the judge bases his conclusions on what was reasonable. How would the reasonable man react to the action committed by the accused? Although Professor Gluckman does not imply that this is what a normal man would want to do, yet the realistic man is very much the normal man whom I am describing. This method of judgment is really what normal people would expect in a normal society. It is the attribute of reasonable or normal human

[1] Gluckman, M. *The Judicial Process among the Barotse of Northern Rhodesia* (1955). Manchester University Press for the Rhodes Livingstone Institute.

beings, and how a normal person views what is right and wrong.

What impresses me so much in African society is the quiet serene behaviour of its men and women—their composure and pleasant personality. The traditional African is never loud, never boastful. In his book *The Ancient Gods* Professor James[2] mentions the quiet man as the outstanding feature of Egyptian personality about 4,000 or 5,000 years ago. He praises the culture that produced this type of person. May we not be witnessing the same personality in Africa today? The quiet man of Egypt and of the Fertile Crescent is indeed the quiet African of today.

When historians stress the greatness of Grecian and Egyptian culture we must not forget that the preternatural was accepted by these great peoples. The whole of Greece believed in the Oracles, in exorcism and in divination. Although their culture was in advance of the rest of the world they believed in the existence of evil spirits ever ready to penetrate their homes and destroy them. The Romans had similar beliefs. The Greeks and Romans contributed to world knowledge in spite of their belief in witchcraft, so it cannot be said that the lack of progress, according to European standards, in African culture is entirely due to this. Yet is is wrong to consider that this belief does not matter, for, as I have already stressed, it must restrain many from carrying out their ideas. This restraint of course is increased when the religion has a similar effect on the behaviour of the individual. African spiritual beliefs are more static than the Christian religion and tend to induce conformity. The European with his dynamic faith is stirred to help others and move towards better things and as soon as he saw the African living under natural conditions assumed his was a backward race. No one doubted that he was primitive. Until recently social anthropologists referred to the tribesmen as primitive. All the nations of Europe looked upon them as backward, primitive and even barbaric. But they were not content to leave them in this situation. The conscience of Christian Europe was

[2] James, E. O. *The Ancient Gods* (1960). Weidenfeld and Nicolson, London.

touched and men with missionary zeal felt obliged to try to uplift the souls of these people. Even if they were not equal to the European they had souls and these could be saved. And so there was an influx of well-wishers to Africa. Missionary stations were set up and hundreds of brave Christians perished on account of the tropical climate and its diseases. Admittedly there were other reasons for the settlement of Africa, both economic and political, but no one can deny or underestimate the Christian motive for coming to this continent. Unfortunately few missionaries thought to find out whether the African had a religion and if he gave the matter momentary consideration soon came to the conclusion that it was mere ancestor worship and witchcraft. And so these men and women gave their devoted services to the African who, on the whole, saw no reason to change his religion or his ritual. None the less, a large number were converted. Not only did the missionaries preach the Gospel, they also set up schools and hospitals in their attempt to uplift the African and in this way were of great material benefit to the people.

With the advance of Africa many students of African life and culture have seen that the African is capable and shows ability and promise and that, given the opportunity, and relieved of the fear of witchcraft there can be no doubt that he will take his place among the other nations of the world. While I can see great virtues in African spiritual belief, I think the African nations cannot afford to be bound by conformity, but should pursue one which encourages change and dynamism while at the same time teaching the same virtues already so carefully inculcated by the Shona faith. While the Shona religion has much of value, I feel that it forces man to follow too closely the example set up by his ancestors and cannot give what the world today demands—what we have come to term 'progress'.

INDEX

This index contains many Shona words and their English equivalents and thus, to some extent, serves as a glossary.

A

additional wives, duties of, 39–40
adultery, 14, 15, 45
Africa, 15, 32, 45, 54, 57, 60, 67
African Studies, 54
Amai (mother), 13
ambuya (grandmother), 13, 74
Amoo, J. W.A., 15
Ancestral spirits, see *vadzimu*
Ancient Gods, The, 127
Aquinas, T., 124
aunt, see *vatete*

B

baba (father), 74
badza (hoe), 27
bakwa (platform), 26
bandauto (ox), 85
Bantu Philosophy, 107
Beattie, J. H., 56, 57
beauty, 121
behaviour pattern, 13
binza, 80
bovora (leaves of vegetables), 8
boy, training of, 65–7
bridewealth, 10, 42, 44, 61, and see *roora*
brother, younger, duties of, 28

C

Chaka, 126
charity, 100
chidao, 47
child, H. F., 55, 60, 74
children, desire for, 19–20
chimbiya (small clay pot), 28
chionono (last pot of beer), 73
chiredzwa (ox or cow), 41

Chisi (day of rest), 5
chowe (bundle of wood), 26
Christianity, 5, 18, ch. 10, 124 et seq.
clapping of hands, 34, 62 et seq.
compensation, 86–8
confession, 91–3
Creator, see *Mwari, Mlimo*
crops, 8
culture, 102 et seq.
Culwick, G. M., 32, 67

D

Daignault, Father, 1
daka (earth), 51
danga (cattle-pen), 7
dangwe (eldest son), 28
dare (meeting-place), 7, 22, 23, 38, 40, 50, etc.
daughter, training of, 67–70
death, 10
demo (axe), 28
dengu (large basket), 39
dibu (trap), 25
Dietherlen, G., 108
discipline, 11, 73
disobedience, 17
disrespect, 17
divorce, 45
dombo, 47
dota (ashes), 51
dovi (monkey-nut relish), 36
dura (grain-bin), 43
duties
    additional wives, 39–40
    aunt (*vatete*), 41–2
    brother, younger, 28
    danger of risk in, 22–3
    division of, 21–4

first wives, 37–9
girl, 28–32
male, 24–7
mugariri, 43–4
muroora, 35–7
muzukuru, 40–1
old women, 42–3
son, eldest, 27–8
wife, 33–4

E

elderly, care for, 18
eldest son, duties of, 27–8
European influence on traditional
   life, 25
Evans-Pritchard, E. E., 57

F

family intimacy, 55 et seq.
father, see *baba*
father-in-law, see *tezrara*
fidelity, 44, 45
first wife, duties of, 37–9
friendship, 97–8

G

Gelfand, M., 15
girl, duties of 28–32
   explanation of sex to, 30
Gluckman, Prof. M., 126
God (*Mlimo*), 116
godo (jealousy), 121
gombana (granary), 22
gota (hut), 27, 40
gotwe (youngest daughter), 43
grandfather, see *sekuru*
grandmother, see *amkuya*
greediness, 120
Griauk, M., 108
gasvi (special handclap), 64
gutsa (tree stump), 38

H

hadyana (pot), 27, 36
hama (friendly neighbour), 47
Hannan, Father, 12, 13, 18, 87
hanzvadzi, 13

hanzvadzikomana, 13
hari (pot), 73
hatred, 121
hoka, 47, 48, 52
homa (wooden ball), 26
honesty (*kurumbisika*), 120
Howman, R., 121
hozi (storeroom), 43
humility, 96–7
hurudza, 48
huta (bow), 28

I

imba (hut), 7, 22, 27, 34–5, 38, etc.
initiation rites, 32–3
insila, 45
intolerance, 91–3

J

James, E. O., 127
jangano, 48
jan-heinz, J., 108
Jealousy, 120
jira, 53
joking relationship, 55–9
Judicial Process among the Barotse, 126

K

Kagame, A., 108
kasakura (weed), 29
kaserima (small hoe), 29
kindness, 120
kissing, 122
kubobodza (clap hands), 71
kugarira (wait for), 44
kugumbatirana (embrace), 62
kukohwa (harvesting), 48
kumbu-ndirana (shaking hands), 62
kunoneka, 71
kupfugama (kneel), 67
kuroora (marriage), 80, 82–6
Kuruma (March), 38
kusakura (weeding), 48
kusungira, 85
kutaura makuhwa (scandal), 121

kuteya mariva (rats), 26
kutsanangura (preciseness), 88–9
kuuchira (greeting), 71

L

language, 102 et seq.
  disrespectful, 18
Laws, R., 1
Livingstone, Dr. D., 1
love, 120

M

mahumbe (trial marriage), 31–2
makunguo (crows), 38
male,
    duties of, 24–7
    supremacy of, 14–16
mamere (fermented grain), 37
Man, 98
manners, 60 et seq.
mapfihwa (hearthstones), 40
mapfunde (grain), 39
maputiro (upbringing), 80
marriage, 6, 8, and see *kuroora*
masungiro, 31, 43, 58
matanda (large piece of wood), 26
mbezo (adze), 25
mbeu (seed), 38
mbiya (relish pot), 81
mharadzi, 119
mharadzo (last pot of beer), 48, 73
mhararano (paths), 84
mhondoro (tribal spirits), 5, 47, 77, 94, 110
mhunga (bulrush millet), 8, 39
migoti (cooking sticks), 27
misere (arrows), 28
mkukwe (sleeping-mat), 70, 84
Mlimo, 116
mnyoku (disease), 92
Moffat, R., 1
mombe (beast), 37, 41, 52, 53
mombe yechishava, 31
mombe youmai (spirit of mother), 10
morals, 44–5
mudzimu (ancestral spirit), 19
mugariri, duties of, 43–4
mugwako (spoon), 25
muhacha, 38
mukaranga (second wife), 38

mukokeri, 73
mukombe (first pot of beer), 73
mukona, 13
mukosi (string of beads), 51
mukuwasha (son-in-law), 13, 41
mumera, 39
Munday, J. T., 60, 100
mundya (cloth), 31
Muntu—an outline of Neo-African culture, 108
munynguna, 13
munyai (intermediary), 47, 59, 76, 82–3
mupini (axe-handle), 25
muranda, 47
muroora (eldest son's wife), 35–7, 74
muroyi (witch), 50, 94, 121
musha (group of huts), 7
musika (whisk), 27
musonyi (cross-cousins), 56
mutorwa (stranger), 21
mutupo (totem), 69
muzukuru (nephew), 13, 33, 62
    duties of, 40–1
mwana, 13
Mwari, 115
mweni (visitor), 70
mwoyochena (kindness), 120

N

Native Affairs Department Annual, 44, 55, 60, 74, 98, 108, 121
ndarira (bangle), 35, 51, 79, 81
ndiro (plate), 25, 28
nephew, see *muzukuru*
newly wedded wives, 35–7
ngana (diviner), 75, 86, 87, 91 et seq.
nganga (medicine man), 5, 53
ngozi (angered spirit), 17
nhava (fibre bag), 40
nhimbe, 47–8
nhindiri (a game), 27
nhumbi (pledge), 59, 82
nyali, 56

O

old women, duties of, 42–3
ownership of property, 11

P

parents, love for, 16–18
patience, 89–90
pfuma (part of bridewealth), 82, 83
'playing hard to get', 59
preciseness, 88–9
procedure, 72 et seq.

R

Radcliffe-Brown, A. R., 57
Read, M., 44, 57, 60, 66
reciprocation, 78
ripira mhosva, 99
ritual sacrifices, 23
roora (bridewealth), 30, 43, 44, 76
rudo (love), 120
rukukwe (mat), 25
rukweza (millet), 39, 48, 79
ruvengo (hatred), 121
ruware (rock), 39

S

sabuka (headman), 8, 48, 73
sadza (porridge), 29, 34, 51, 67, 68, 84
sahwira, 47, 49 et seq.
scandal, 121
Schweitzer, Dr. A., 1
sekuru (grandfather), 9, 10, 28, 41, 74
seniority, 12–14
Serritus, M., 124
sexes, separation of, 21 et seq.
sexual intercourse before marriage,
   32–3, 44, 67
sharing, 98–9
Shamwari, 46–7
shiri (birds), 26
Shona Religion, 15, 58
Shona Ritual, 58
Simmons, D. C., 32
Sloan, A., 67
son, eldest, duties of, 27–8
spirits, see *mhondoro*, *vadzima*
status of individual, 9–10; and see
   'seniority' and 'duties'
Stewart, J., 1
svikiro (medium), 5
svingo (wood), 26

T

Tempels, Fr. Placide, 107 et seq.
Tew, M., 54, 58
tezvara (father-in-law), 13, 47, 58, 79,
   83, 85
'to the end', 101
tsaiya (pot), 27, 80
tsanga (reeds), 25
tsenda (sharp end of adze), 25
tsito (fire), 25
tsvimbo yehoma (a game), 26
tswande (basket), 25, 27

U

umsindo, 45
upfu (meal), 39
Usahwira, 48–55
utani (friend), 54

V

vadzimu (ancestral spirits), 24, 27, 30,
   35, 77, 94, 110, 114, 115
vahosi, 37–9, 40
vakuwasha (relations by marriage), 46,
   58
vambuya (mother-in-law), 13, 14, 58
vamwene (mother-in-law), 37
vanakomana (sister's son), 40
vanasikana (sister's daughter), 40
varamu (wife's sister), 23
vasekura, 13
vatete (aunt), 41–2, 62, 74
vatorwa (strangers), 7
vazukuru (sister's children), 40, 46
virginity, 14, 30, 45, 76, 80
visitors, reception of, 70

W

White, C. M. N., 58
wife
      additional, 39–40
      duties of, 33–4
      first, 37–9
      newly wedded, see *muroora*
Wilson, G., 60
witchcraft, 94 et seq., 119, 128

Z

zimbe (embers), 25, 65
zunde (field), 22, 58.